MW01644028

The Final Betrayal

A Cautionary Tale

How Technocracy Destroyed America

Patrick M. Wood
Courtenay Turner

Coherent Publishing, LLC

Copyright © 2025 Patrick M. Wood and Courtenay Turner

All rights reserved.

ISBN: 979-8-9935646-0-9

No portion of this book may be reproduced in any form without written permission from the publisher or author, except as permitted by U.S. copyright law.

For the would-be plebes who
thought that we were home free.

Contents

Introduction

In the days following the election of Donald J. Trump on November 2, 2024, there was an explosion of Technocrats swarming all over Washington, DC. Even before the inauguration on January 23, 2025, this "shock and awe" campaign left people scratching their heads: "What just happened here?"

The Department of Government Efficiency (DOGE) was already staffed and waiting to pounce on day one after the inauguration. Elon Musk had already called for Technocrats to come to his aid to secure the data flows from primary agencies like:

- Office of Personnel Management
- General Services Administration
- Social Security Administration
- Treasury Department
- United States Digital Service
- Centers for Medicare & Medicaid Services
- Department of Defense
- Commerce Department
- Department of Energy
- Health and Human Services

- Department of Labor
- Veterans Affairs, among others (Desser 2025).

By February 13, just two weeks into the Administration, 3.2 percent of the federal workforce (77,000 workers) had already accepted buyout offers to leave. According to Axios, this was short of the original goal of 5-10 percent. (Rubin 2025). Another 58,500 federal employees have been directly fired. The Administration is planning a total reduction of 275,000, or 11.5 percent, by the end of 2025.

We will cover this more extensively in Chapter 4.

In short, the Technocrats have set up a permanent camp in Washington, DC. From a high-level view, we assert that there was a coup d'état that nobody, but nobody, ever voted on or asked for just a few months earlier. We need to dig deeper.

At the Drop of a Hat

Some of you will remember when Elon Musk trotted on stage in October 2024, sporting a Black MAGA and declaring, “I’m not just MAGA, I’m Dark MAGA”. What on earth was he talking about?

Well, Dark MAGA as a meme first started on Twitter on January 21, 2022. Thereafter, it was promoted by alt-right figures in support of Donald Trump. There were conflicting currents that included some QAnon themes, authoritarian typology, and even some Nazi symbology. But all of that was crowded out when the Dark Enlightenment overpowered Dark MAGA.

Musk’s adoption of the black MAGA hat and meme aesthetics was widely read as a wink to those “in the know”—tech elite and radical new right circles who understand the Dark Enlightenment undercurrents beneath the meme. (Stall 2022)

What is the Dark Enlightenment? Although we will cover it in more detail in Chapters Two and Five, suffice it to say that this is where we were bamboozled.

The Dark Enlightenment is the polar opposite of the MAGA movement. It is anti-democratic, anti-freedom, anti-liberty, anti-human, and thoroughly technocratic. Behind it is a twisted philosophy created by a TechBro from Silicon Valley named Curtis Yarvin. Since he started writing in 2007, he has captured the mind and soul of Silicon Valley — and in particular, those of Peter Thiel and Elon Musk. Consider some highlights:

- Views Democracy, Constitutional Government, and Populism as inherently flawed and must be overthrown
- Endorses rule by an unelected centralized sovereign, i.e., a CEO, or a Monarch
- Promotes Technocratic governance by unelected and unaccountable officials
- The government should be run as a profit-seeking "Sov-Corp" that would own or control all the assets in society
- Promotes Accelerationism: The existing system is not worth reforming and should be allowed, or even forced, to unravel quickly to make way for a new order.

As a block, all the Technocrats in Washington, DC, embrace Dark Enlightenment philosophy. As such, they are traitors to the MAGA movement, the Constitution, and our government.

Trump's Actions Speak Louder Than Words

The populist MAGA movement elected President Trump with high expectations for radical transformation: reversing globalism, restoring economic and cultural primacy, and confronting institutional elites. For millions of Americans, Trump represented the light at the end of the tunnel, the last hope of restoring America to its former days.

For all of the good things accomplished so far, they pale in comparison to the permanent advancement of Technocracy in just the first six months of the Administration. None of this was seen in advance, much less through the lens of the Dark Enlightenment.

The major initiatives thus far include the unregulated advancement of AI, building infrastructure for AI data centers, and the creation of a privatized system of cryptocurrency as an alternative to central bank digital currency. This will be covered in detail in Chapters 8 and 9.

The Government as a Startup Company?

All of a sudden, you saw the concept of **accelerationism** applied to government. Usually, this is a term commonly used to describe a startup company in Silicon Valley. Mark Zuckerberg, for instance, perfectly encapsulated this concept in the late 2000s with the phrase, "*Move fast and break things. Unless you are breaking stuff, you are not moving fast enough.*"

Since then, accelerationism has been further defined as the belief that intensifying the contradictions, dysfunction, or technologies of the present will bring about more rapid—and radical—systemic change, for better or worse. Further, it justifies actions or rhetoric that push a society, economy, or system toward crisis, believing that only through such rupture are new forms of organization or order possible.

Since Trump took office, this has been the driving force of change with organizations like DOGE, which was ostensibly run by Elon Musk. Put another way, Technocrats are fully intent on running America into the ditch, not making it great again. Can we repeat Zuckerberg? "*Move fast and break things. Unless you are breaking stuff, you are not moving fast enough.*"

MAGA never, ever dreamed that America would (so quickly) be taken over by a bunch of lunatic Technocrats intent on destroying the country.

All of this adds up to BETRAYAL and TREACHERY. It adds up to TREASON. Worse, we are left with the memory and love of a nation that once existed but will never exist again.

Yes, we have been bamboozled for the last time.

References

Desser, Chas, All the Federal Agencies DOGE Has Gotten Access To, Intelligencer, Feb 10, 2025. (https://nymag.com/intelligencer/article/doge-elon-musk-what-federal-agencies-access-lawsuits.html)

Rubin, April, Trump administration falls short of federal workforce buyout goal, Axios, Feb 13, 2025 (https://www.axios.com/2025/02/13/trump-buyout-federal-workforce-deadline-goal)

Shao, Elena; Wu, Ashley. "The Federal Work Force Cuts So Far, Agency by Agency". The New York Times, June 3, 2025. (https://www.nytimes.com/interactive/2025/03/28/us/politics/trump-doge-federal-job-cuts.html)

Stall and Grober, An Assessment of the Dark MAGA Trend in Far-Right Online Spaces, Global Network on Extremism & Technology, April 5, 2022. (https://gnet-research.org/2022/04/05/from-orange-to-red-an-assessment-of-the-dark-maga-trend-in-far-right-online-spaces/)

Chapter 1

The Rise of Technocracy

All of the TechBros who have invaded DC since the November 2024 election are properly called Technocrats. They are unelected and unaccountable. Most Americans have never heard of people like David Sacks, Thomas Shedd, Lynne Parker, Emil Michael, or Alexei Bulazel, all of whom are Technocrats. There are many more that you will never know about because their names are hidden behind the wall of national security.

Yet, these are the people who are actively betraying America while turning it into a Technocratic state.

Consider: In just eleven months since the inauguration, these brainiacs have constructed a new crypto-centric financial system and bolted in AI to run major sections of the Administration. Further, they influenced legislation and Executive Orders to deregulate AI and hamstring the states from interfering.

This was all done in the light of accelerationism, within the framework of the Dark Enlightenment: "*Move fast and break things. Unless you are breaking stuff, you are not moving fast enough.*" (Mark Zuckerberg)

Where did these people come from in the first place? Where did this mechanistic worldview originate? The answer might surprise you.

The Roots of Technocracy

Technocracy has a long and well-defined history. When a group of engineers and scientists got together at Columbia University in 1932 to design a brand new resource-centric economic system, they thought that capitalism was dead. They saw themselves as the saviors of society. Rational citizens quickly realized how hare-brained the whole scheme was.

In 1937, the movement described itself like this:

> *Technocracy is the science of social engineering, the scientific operation of the entire social mechanism to produce and distribute goods and services to the entire po pulation... For the first time in human history, it will be done as a scientific, technical, and engineering problem. There will be no place for Politics, Politicians, Finance or Financiers, Rackets or Racketeers... Technocracy will distribute by means of a certificate of distribution available to every citizen from birth to death. (Editor 1937)*

Think about this:

- The Science of Social Engineering – messing with your mind

- They would make all decisions to manufacture and distribute goods

- All decisions would be made by science

- All politicians would be fired on the spot

- Finance would be replaced with energy credits via Universal Basic Income payments.

- You would get your certificate of distribution from birth to death.

The *Technocracy Study Course,* written as the bible of Technocracy in 1934, gave some background:

Technocracy is dealing with social phenomena in the widest sense of the word; this includes not only actions of human beings, but also everything which directly or indirectly affects their actions. Consequently, the studies of technocracy embrace practically the whole field of science and industry. Biology, climate, natural resources, and industrial equipment all enter into the social picture. (Hubbert 1934)

Their clear plan was to take over biology, climate, natural resources, and industrial equipment. This is the modern essence of the United Nations' programs of Agenda 21, 2030 Agenda, and Sustainable Development.

Technocrats wanted to dump the price-based monetary system (dollars) in favor of energy credits. Every citizen would be issued an allotment at the beginning of a period to spend on goods and services.

Necessary Requirements For Technocracy

Engineers are disciplined to list the requirements of every project, and Technocracy was no exception. However, only seven requirements were listed, which was a testament to their ingenuity:

1. Register on a continuous 24-hour-per-day basis the total net conversion of energy

There were two reasons to keep track of usable energy: First, it was the basis for issuing "energy script" to all citizens for buying and selling goods and services. Second, it predicted economic activity because all such activity is directly dependent upon energy. (Note that Technocrats intended to pre-determine how much energy would be made available in the first place.)

2. By means of the registration of energy converted and consumed, make possible a balanced load

Once available energy was quantified, it was to be allocated to consumers and manufacturers so as to limit production and consumption. Technocrats would have control of both ends, so that everything is managed according to their scientific formulas.

The modern Smart Grid, with its ubiquitous WiFi-enabled Smart Meters on homes and businesses, is the exact fulfillment of these two requirements. The concept of "energy web" was first revitalized in 1999 by the Bonneville Power Authority (BPA) in Portland, Oregon.

3. Provide a continuous inventory of all production and consumption

Technocrats were obsessed with aggregating inventory quantities in the economic system from beginning to end. Inventory would be stored in production facilities until it was ready to be delivered to consumers and producers. Only actual consumption by end-users would shrink inventory.

We see this concept used extensively in modern corporations, termed Supply Chain Management (SCM), where its goal is to minimize stored inventory (squeezing out the inefficiencies) and make for "just-in-time" manufacturing and consumption.

4. Provide a specific registration of the type, kind, etc., of all goods and services, where produced and where used

This granular level of data tracking drills down to specific items and would ostensibly assign a trackable serial number to every item manufactured, shipped and ultimately consumed by individuals or other manufacturing processes. Such detailed item tracking is a core value of modern Supply Chain Management theory and practice.

The greatest enabler of Technocracy is the Internet of Things (IoT), where all connected devices are networked together via the latest 5G wireless technology. Tom Wheeler, former head of the FCC, praised 5G and the IoT in 2017: **"If something can be connected, it will be connected".** The harvesting of data from billions of sensors embedded in the IoT will, for the first time in history, provide real-time data collection. In turn, this data flow will put wind in the sails of Artificial Intelligence algorithms designed to control society.

5. Provide specific registration of the consumption of each individual, plus a record and description of the individual

This requirement is a cross-check of inventory against actual consumption by a verified individual. Thus, if something is bought but not consumed immediately, the Technocrat overlords could take action to stop such behavior. It must be understood that Technocracy intended to entirely eliminate private property, savings, and inheritance, among other things. The hoarding of consumable items was viewed as unauthorized savings.

The means of collecting this information is through monitoring and total surveillance. Surveillance and data collection are seen everywhere today, and according to Technocrats, there is no such thing as "enough" data. The Intelligence agencies (NSA, CIA, DHS, etc.) are creating massive national databases that harvest real-time data from every conceivable source. Surveillance includes biometric data (i.e., facial scans, DNA, iris and voice scans), communications (email, phone calls), financial transactions, location tracking (geospatial intel), social media, psychographic data, etc.

6. Allow the citizen the widest latitude of choice in consuming his individual share of Continental physical wealth

First, there would not be a wide range of selection of goods and services because there would be no competition between manufacturers. Products would be designed and manufactured by

Technocrats at their sole discretion. The real thing in view here is the aggregate amount of "Continental physical wealth" and how much of it you deserve to consume. Technocrats largely view humans as so many cattle in a feed lot, existing only to be fed a managed diet from birth to death, housed and shielded from the weather, medically treated for maximum efficiency, etc.

7. Distribute goods and services to every member of the population

The key to this last requirement is that Technocrats demanded that every single person in the Technate would be forced to participate. Like today, outliers were not to be allowed. For instance, the tagline "No person left behind" is seen throughout the UN's literature on Sustainable Development. (Wood 2022)

The Trilateral Commission: Rockefeller & Brzezinski

In 1973, David Rockefeller teamed up with Zbigniew Brzezinski to start the Trilateral Commission to create a "New International Economic Order" (NIEO). Brzezinski was a professor of political science at Columbia University when he wrote *Between Two Ages: America's Role in the Technetronic Era*. This resonated with Rockefeller, then Chairman of Chase Manhattan Bank, as a way to convert his cash wealth into resource wealth.

By early 1974, Rockefeller had fed the NIEO concept to the United Nations under the guise of U.N. Resolution 3201, DECLARATION ON THE ESTABLISHMENT OF A NEW INTERNATIONAL ECONOMIC ORDER and Resolution 3202, PROGRAMME OF ACTION ON THE ESTABLISHMENT OF A NEW INTERNATIONAL ECONOMIC ORDER.

By the time Jimmy Carter and Walter Mondale were elected in 1976, both had been appointed as members of the Trilateral Commission. Brzezinski was appointed as National Security Advisor and proceeded to stack the Cabinet with other Trilaterals. By their own admission, they were not interested in a political takeover, but rather in dominating the driving force of all global economic activity to ensure the birth of the New International Economic Order. (Wood, 1981)

Just 10 years later, a European member of the Trilateral Commission was appointed to head the U.N. World Commission on Environment and Development. Gro Harlem Brundtland, formerly the Prime Minister of Norway, became known as the "Mother of Sustainable Development" (Jeracki 2016) when she wrote *Our Common Future* in 1987.

The U.N. unveiled the master plan at the Earth Summit (formally, the U.N. Conference on Environment and Development) held in Rio De Janeiro in 1992, which produced the infamous *Agenda 21* action plan that was immediately signed by 178 nations.

All said, *Agenda 21* was created and scripted by the Trilateral Commission from start to finish. It was modeled after historic Technocracy, a resource-based economic system.

Today, we see a horde of Technocrats who have descended on Washington, DC, to claim the fruit of their labor. In short, we have come full circle to Brzezinski's original vision for "America's Role in the Technetronic Era."

References

Editor, Technocrat Magazine, 1937.

Hubbert & Scott, Technocracy Study Course, Technocracy, Inc., 1934.

Kate Jeracki, "Mother of Sustainablity Kicks off Women's History Month", Colorado State University, 2016. (https://source.colostate.edu/mother-of-sustainability-to-speak-at-colorado-state-university/)

Wood, Patrick, "Technocracy's Necessary Requirements", Technocracy News & Trends, December 16, 2022. (https://www.technocracy.news/day-6-technocracy-and-total-surveillance/)

Wood, Patrick and Sutton, Antony, *Trilaterals Over Washington, Volumes I and II,* 1980.

Chapter 2

Peter Thiel, Architect

Behind every coup d'état and revolution, there is an architect. A mastermind. A strategist. A hidden hand. A puppet-master.

To call Peter Thiel the betrayer-in-chief of the American populist movement misses the point. MAGA brought the "useful idiots" to the table. They were pawns in a bigger game, seen as mere fodder for the cannons of destruction leveled at America.

The objective was to launch the king into position to declare "checkmate" for Technocracy.

The chess analogy is appropriate. Peter Thiel was an avid and fiercely competitive chess player who started at age six and continued through his days at Stanford University. He rose to become one of the top junior chess players in the United States, earning the title of US Chess Federation Life Master. (Nathan 2023) He didn't just win; he sought to trounce his opponents.

Chess teaches you to think ahead several moves to outwit your opponent, without tipping him off to your own strategy.

But Thiel got a revelation after working for a major law firm after graduation: "competition is for losers." Reid Hoffman revealed Thiel's new life strategy in a podcast:

> *Competition will make you, at best, a winner in a losing game. If you really want to scale a business, escape the competition. Change the playing field. Hang up your jersey. This applies to businesses as well as individuals. Don't try to beat the competitors at their own game. You have to invent a new game—and master it. (Hoffman 2025)*

This became the guiding principle for all of Theil's business creations and investments: PayPal, Palantir, Facebook, SpaceX, LinkedIn, Yelp, Airbnb, Stripe, Spotify, etc. Each of these companies invented a new game and then mastered it, eventually reaching monopoly status - in other words, "escaping the competition."

A New Game To Dominate America

Peter Thiel invented a new game to capture America, and didn't share his strategy with anyone along the way. Why should he? He alone mastered it. He is trouncing all wannabe competitors who don't know the rules of the game, including politicians, MAGA, and pundits.

In the shadowy corridors of Silicon Valley, where innovation masks ambition and technology veils control, Peter Thiel stands as the quintessential architect of the technocratic betrayal. Born in 1967 in Frankfurt, Germany, and raised in the United States, Thiel co-founded PayPal in 1998, revolutionizing online payments before selling it to eBay for $1.5 billion in 2002.

He established Palantir Technologies in 2003, a data analytics firm deeply intertwined with government surveillance and intelligence agencies, and Founders Fund in 2005, a venture capital firm that has backed disruptive technologies from SpaceX to Airbnb (Foroohar 2019).

Thiel's estimated net worth exceeds $26 billion according to Bloomberg, but his true currency is influence—wielded through a network of protégés, investments, and ideological alliances that have infiltrated the highest echelons of the Trump administration (Forbes 2025). As the financial backer of Curtis Yarvin's Urbit project since 2013 and a vocal critic of democracy, Thiel embodies the Dark Enlightenment's disdain for populist governance, viewing it as incompatible with true progress and freedom (Kaufman 2025).

> *I must confess that over the last two decades, I have changed radically on the question of how to achieve these goals. Most importantly, I no longer believe that freedom and democracy are compatible. By tracing out the development of my thinking, I hope to frame some of the challenges faced by all classical liberals today. (Thiel, 2009)*

His protégé, Vice President J.D. Vance—whom Thiel employed at Mithril Capital and bankrolled with over $15 million for his 2022 Senate campaign—serves as a direct conduit for Thiel's anti-democratic vision into the White House (Pequeno 2024). Through Palantir's lucrative contracts with the Department of Defense and immigration enforcement agencies, amassing over $113 million in federal deals by mid-2025, Thiel has positioned himself as the unseen hand guiding the administration's accelerationist agenda: deregulating AI, slashing federal bureaucracies via DOGE, and advancing surveillance technologies that erode personal liberties (Trefis Team 2025).

This chapter unveils Thiel's strategic playbook, a set of ten covert principles that have propelled him from tech entrepreneur to the de facto shadow sovereign, orchestrating the subversion of MAGA's promises into a monopolistic, technocratic dystopia. While it's worth acknowledging there may be puppeteers above him, blunting operational success requires targeting the hands we can see.

Thiel's Playbook: Ten Hidden Rules for Absolute Domination

Beneath Thiel's public persona as a libertarian visionary lies a meticulously crafted set of strategies, disguised as business acumen but rooted in a philosophy that prioritizes elite control over democratic chaos. These principles, inferred from his actions, writings like *Zero to One* (Thiel, 2014), and political maneuvers, form the backbone of his influence. They are not overtly proclaimed—true to their nature—but evident in how he has built empires, placed allies, and reshaped institutions.

As we dissect them, the betrayal becomes clear: Thiel's rules are tools for dismantling the very freedoms MAGA sought to restore, replacing them with a sovereign corporation where power is monopolized by the few. A chess master who achieved the USCF National Master title in 1992 with a peak rating of over 2200—placing him in the top percentile of players worldwide—Thiel's strategic prowess on the board mirrors his real-world maneuvers, anticipating opponents' moves layers deep to secure unchallenged dominance (Chess.com 2025). This sets the stage for viewing his actions through the lens of chess strategy.

Rule #1 - Make up your own rules

Thiel has always operated outside conventional boundaries, inventing frameworks that suit his ambitions rather than adhering to established norms. In founding PayPal, he navigated regulatory gray areas around online finance, effectively rewriting the rules of digital transactions to bypass traditional banking oversight (Chafkin 2021). This ethos extended to his political engagements; in 2016, Thiel became one of the first Silicon Valley titans to endorse Donald Trump, defying the tech industry's progressive consensus and creating his own playbook for "conservative" tech alignment (Sydell 2016). By 2025, this rule manifests in his indirect shaping of the Trump administration's policies, such as advocating for executive overreach in DOGE's workforce reductions, which echo his disdain for bureaucratic "rules" that stifle innovation.

Thiel's philosophy, as articulated in his 2009 Cato Unbound essay, posits that "freedom and democracy are incompatible," allowing him to justify crafting autocratic alternatives free from voter input (Thiel 2009). This self-made governance model is the foundation of his influence, enabling him to impose technocratic order on a chaotic republic—much like a chess master who redefines the opening to trap an opponent early.

Rule #2 - Rules must be hidden

Transparency is the enemy of control in Thiel's world; his strategies thrive in obscurity. While publicly championing libertarian ideals, Thiel has covertly funded anti-democratic thinkers like Curtis Yarvin, investing $1.1 million in Yarvin's Tlon Corporation for the Urbit platform—a decentralized network that mirrors neoreactionary hierarchies without overt political branding (Heathen 2024). In politics, this rule is evident in his "schizophrenic" approach to donations: after pledging no contributions in 2024, Thiel quietly resumed funding Republican causes in 2025, including House races to secure congressional majorities for Trump's agenda, all while denying a full-time role in the administration (Metzger 2025).

His network's infiltration—placing over a dozen allies in key positions from the Office of Science and Technology Policy to HHS—remains veiled, allowing Thiel to pull strings without accountability (Alexander 2025). This concealment disguises his motives, presenting technocratic overhauls as mere efficiency drives rather than steps toward sovereign corporatism, akin to a concealed pawn structure in chess that masks an impending attack.

Rule #3 - Motives must be disguised

Thiel masters the art of misdirection, cloaking authoritarian ambitions in the language of innovation and patriotism. His support for Trump in 2016 was framed as a blow against globalism, yet it advanced his own interests in surveillance tech, for which he appears to have global aspirations; Palantir's contracts surged under the first Trump term, enabling data-mining tools used for immigration enforcement and predictive policing (Peterson 2019).

Similarly, Thiel's investment in Clearview AI, a facial recognition company that scraped over three billion images from the internet to build a database for law enforcement, was presented as a tool for public safety, yet it fueled mass surveillance and privacy violations, aligning with his vision of centralized control (Heathen 2024). Thiel's disdain for transparency as a principle further reveals this deception.

He waged a multi-year vendetta against Gawker, covertly funding lawsuits against the outlet and only admitting his role after bankrupting it in 2016, demonstrating that transparency is, for him, a weapon to wield selectively, not a value to uphold (Sorkin 2016). Thiel disguises his accelerationist push—hastening systemic collapse for rebuilding under elite rule—as "patriotic" investment, such as doubling down on defense tech amid U.S. involvement in global conflicts (Grifith and Metz 2025).

His mentorship of Vance, portrayed as nurturing young talent, installs a loyalist to echo Dark Enlightenment tenets like RAGE (Retire All Government Employees), rebranded as DOGE's cost-cutting crusade (Beauchamp 2019). This disguise betrays MAGA's anti-elite rhetoric, as Thiel's true motive—centralized power—undermines the movement from within, reflecting the feints and decoys of a chess master diverting attention from the real threat.

Rule #4 - Redefine the language

Thiel excels at semantic engineering, twisting terms to align with his vision. In *Zero to One*, he redefines "competition" as destructive, urging entrepreneurs to seek monopolies instead—a linguistic shift that justifies anti-competitive practices like Palantir's dominance in government data analytics (Thiel and Masters 2014). He further redefines "progress" not as incremental improvements but as singular, disruptive acts of creation, stating, "Every time we create something new, we go from 0 to 1. The act of creation is singular, as is the moment of creation, and the result is something fresh and strange" (Thiel and Masters 2014).

This framing elevates his ventures like Palantir and Founders Fund as revolutionary, while dismissing competitive markets as stagnant. Similarly, Thiel splits "optimism" into "definite" and "indefinite" variants, promoting the former—planned, actionable belief in a better future—over vague hope, arguing, "Definite optimism works when you build the future you envision" (Thiel and Masters 2014).

This critique of passive optimism justifies his secretive, high-stakes investments in tech monopolies. To seduce intellectual elites, Thiel adopts Tolkien-inspired metaphors from Curtis Yarvin, endorsing the "dark elf" narrative where reactionary intellectuals (like himself) ally with "hobbits" (conservative populists) to undermine progressive "high elves," casting his anti-democratic agenda as a mythic struggle for a new order (Yarvin 2022).

He further weaves historical analogies, invoking thinkers like Machiavelli and Carlyle, to frame his technocratic vision as a return to natural hierarchies, masking authoritarianism as intellectual destiny (Packer 2011). Politically, he aligns with Yarvin and the Neoractionaries, reframing "democracy" as inefficiency, proposing "monarchy" or CEO-rule as efficient alternatives, influencing Vance's calls to,

> *seize the administrative state for our purposes...fire every single mid-level bureaucrat every civil servant in the administrative State replace them with our people and when the courts because you will get taken to court and then when the courts stop you... Say the chief justice has made his ruling, now let him enforce it...* (Vance 2021).

This rule aids the current administration's narrative: mass firings are "efficiency," AI surveillance is "security," and cryptocurrency promotion is "financial freedom," masking the erosion of private property and civil liberties (Pogue 2025). Thiel's redefinition obscures the technocratic coup, turning betrayal into "progress," much as a chess player renames a gambit to unsettle an adversary.

Rule #5 - Insert a trusted mole

Strategic infiltration is Thiel's hallmark; he plants loyalists to advance his agenda covertly. J.D. Vance, hired by Thiel in 2017 and funded for his political ascent, now serves as Vice President, pushing policies like deregulating AI and gutting federal agencies—direct echoes of Thiel's views (Mac, Schleifer 2024). Other moles include Thiel alumni in DOGE and the Office of Science and Technology Policy, steering the administration toward surveillance-heavy tech (Dwoskin 2025). This tactic, honed in business through investments in firms like Anduril (defense tech), ensures Thiel's influence permeates without his direct involvement, betraying public trust by embedding private interests in government—paralleling the insertion of a knight deep into enemy territory on the chessboard.

Rule #6 - Place players in strategic positions

Thiel's chess-like planning positions allies for maximum leverage. Beyond Vance, his network includes Elon Musk (early investor in SpaceX) and figures like David Sacks, now in advisory roles, amplifying technocratic policies in the 2025 administration (Vance and Thiel 2024). In tech, funding Yarvin placed neoreactionary ideas in Silicon Valley circles; politically, backing Trump transition team members in 2017 set the stage for 2025's DOGE (Jamison 2025). These placements create a web of influence, turning the White House into a node in Thiel's sovereign network, embodying the positional play of a chess master who controls key squares to dictate the game's flow.

Rule #7 - Balance the playing field

Thiel feigns fairness while tilting scales in his favor. He critiques "woke" progressivism publicly, positioning himself as a balancer against leftist excesses, yet his actions—funding right-wing causes while profiting from government contracts—create imbalances benefiting elites (Somerville, Bergengruen et al). In 2025, this rule appears in Palantir's AI databases, ostensibly "balancing" security needs but enabling mass surveillance. The illusion of equity masks the consolidation of power, similar to maintaining material balance in chess while preparing a devastating imbalance.

Rule #8 - Never compete

Echoing his mantra that "competition is for losers," Thiel avoids direct rivalry, opting for unchallenged dominance. PayPal's early monopoly on online payments set the tone; Palantir's exclusive government deals follow suit (Thiel and Masters 2014). Politically, he sidesteps open contests by influencing from afar. This non-competitive stance, accelerates technocracy's rise, unopposed, like a chess endgame where one side has already secured a winning position without further clashes.

Rule #9 - Plan 5 steps ahead before making a move

Thiel's foresight is legendary; as a chess master who competed in national tournaments and maintained a FIDE rating of 2199—just one point shy of the Candidate Master title—he anticipates outcomes layers deep, calculating multi-move sequences with precision (Chessgames.com 2024). Investing in Facebook in 2004 foresaw social media's dominance; backing Trump in 2016 positioned him for 2025 gains (Thiel and Masters 2014). His grooming of Vance since 2016—employment, funding, endorsement—culminated in Vance's VP role, enabling long-term policy shifts like cryptocurrency integration. This multi-step planning ensures the Dark Enlightenment's gradual implementation, mirroring the deep calculation that defines master-level chess.

Rule #10 - Always seek monopoly

At the core of Thiel's ethos is monopoly-building, from PayPal's payment gateway to Palantir's data monopoly in intelligence (Chafkin 2021). In politics, he seeks ideological monopoly through NRx alliances, influencing the administration to create a "GovCorp" where technocrats hold unchallenged sway (Land 2012). This manifests in exclusive AI and crypto initiatives, betraying free markets for elite control— the ultimate checkmate in his grand strategy.

Conclusion: The Thiel Betrayal Unveiled

Peter Thiel's ten rules are not mere business tactics; they are weapons in the Dark Enlightenment's arsenal, deployed to subvert America's constitutional foundations. Infused with the strategic depth of his chess mastership, these principles—through hidden motives, strategic placements, and monopolistic pursuits—have engineered a technocratic stronghold in Washington, using figures like Vance to accelerate the unraveling of democracy and trampling on the Constitution. This is the ultimate treason: a billionaire's playbook masquerading as innovation, dooming the republic to corporate monarchy. As Palantir's tendrils deepen and DOGE dismantles, Americans must awaken to this shadow sovereign before the light of liberty is extinguished forever.

References

Alexander, Sophie, "Peter Thiel's Deep Ties to Trump's Top Ranks: The Tech Magnate Has Many Links to the New Trump Administration and the Cost-Slashing Effort by Elon Musk", Bloomberg, March 7, 2025. (https://www.bloomberg.com/features/2025-peter-thiel-trump-administration-connections/)

Beauchamp, Zack, "Accelerationism: The Obscure Idea Inspiring White Supremacist Killers Around the World", Vox, November 18, 2019. (https://www.vox.com/the-highlight/2019/11/11/20882005/accelerationism-white-supremacy-christchurch)

Editor, "Peter A. Thiel", Bloomberg Billionaires Index. 2025. (https://www.bloomberg.com/billionaires/profiles/peter-a-thiel/)

Chafkin, Max, The Contrarian: Peter Thiel and Silicon Valley's Pursuit of Power, New York: Penguin Press, 2021.

Editor, "Peter Thiel Player Profile", Chess.com, 2025. (https://www.chess.com/players/peter-thiel)

Editor, "The Chess Games of Peter Thiel", Chessgames.com, Last updated September 3, 2024. (https://www.chessgames.com/player/peter_thiel.html)

U.S. Department of Defense, "Contracts for May 21, 2025", May 21, 2025. (https://www.defense.gov/News/Contracts/Contract/Article/4194643/)

Chivers, Tom, “Palantir Revenue Tops $1 Billion on Back of AI, Government Contracts”, Semafor, August 5, 2025. (https://www.semafor.com/article/08/04/2025/palantir-revenue-tops-1-billion-on-back-of-ai-government-contracts)

Demarest, Colin, “Palantir’s $10 Billion Army Contract Continues Its D.C. Win Streak”, Axios, August 5, 2025. (https://www.axios.com/2025/08/05/palantir-army-software-contract)

Diehl, Stephen, “Deconstructing the Worldview of Peter Thiel”, February 1, 2023. (https://www.stephendiehl.com/posts/desconstructing_thiel/)

Dwoskin, Elizabeth, “Silicon Valley’s Influence in the New Trump Era”, Washington Post, February 15, 2025.

Dwoskin, Elizabeth, Hannah Natanson, and Jacob Bogage, “In Trump’s Washington, Palantir Is Winning Big: From Warfighting and Tracking Deportations to Writing State Department Cables with AI, the Company Is Benefiting from a New Technology-Driven Cost-Cutting Ethos in Government”, Washington Post, August 1, 2025. (https://www.washingtonpost.com/technology/2025/08/01/palantir-trump-defense-tech-ai-software)

Editor, “Peter Thiel”, Forbes, September 19, 2025. (https://www.forbes.com/profile/peter-thiel/)

Foroohar, Rana, *Don’t Be Evil: How Big Tech Betrayed Its Founding Principles—and All of Us*, New York: Currency, 2019.

Griffith, Erin, and Cade Metz , “A.I. Military Start-Up Anduril Close to Deal That Would Value Company at $28 Billion: The Southern California Start-Up, Which Builds Flying Drones and Missiles, Is Set to Raise Up to $2.5 Billion”, New York Times, February 7, 2025. (https://archive.ph/mwBgx#selection-4395.0-4399.110)

Haywood, Charles, "The Flight 93 Election Revisited", The Worthy House, April 7, 2019. (https://americanmind.org/salvo/the-flight-93-election-revisited/)

Haywood, Charles, Review of After the Flight 93 Election: The Vote That Saved America and What We Still Have to Lose, by Michael Anton, The Worthy House, April 7, 2019. (https://theworthyhouse.com/2019/04/07/book-review-after-the-flight-93-election-the-vote-that-saved-america-and-what-we-still-have-to-lose-michael-anton/)

Heathen, Richard, "Prologue to the Counter Tradition: Neoplatonic Trumpism", Arktos, October 21, 2024. (https://arktos.com/2024/10/21/prologue-to-the-counter-tradition-napoleonic-trumpism/)

Hammond, Samuel, "Peter Thiel's Plan to Become CEO of America", Niskanen Center, August 3, 2016. (https://www.niskanencenter.org/peter-thiels-plan-become-ceo-america/)

Kaufman, Ava, "Curtis Yarvin's Plot Against America: The Reactionary Blogger's Call for a Monarch to Rule the Country Once Seemed Like a Joke. Now the Right Is Ready to Bend the Knee", New Yorker, June 2, 2025. (https://www.newyorker.com/magazine/2025/06/09/curtis-yarvin-profile)

Land, Nick, "The Dark Enlightenment", Self-published essay, 2012. (https://www.thedarkEnlightenment.com/the-dark-enlightenment-by-nick-land/)

Mac, Ryan, and Theodore Schleifer, "How a Network of Tech Billionaires Helped J.D. Vance Leap Into Power: Mr. Vance Spent Less Than Five Years in Silicon Valley's Tech Industry, but the Connections He Made with Peter Thiel and Others Became Crucial to His Political Ascent", New York Times, July 27, 2024. (https://archive.ph/QDY46#selection-555.0-559.167)

Metzger, Bryan, "Peter Thiel's Political Hiatus Is Over. Here's Where His Money's Flowing Now", Business Insider, July 26,

2025. (https://www.businessinsider.com/peter-thiel-spending-money-politics-again-house-republicans-2025-7)

Packer, George, "No Death, No Taxes: The Libertarian Futurism of a Silicon Valley Billionaire", New Yorker, November 28, 2011. (https://www.newyorker.com/magazine/2011/11/28/no-death-no-taxes. https://archive.ph/YevFN)

Pequeno, Antonio, "JD Vance And Peter Thiel: What To Know About The Relationship Between Trump's VP Pick And The Billionaire", Forbes, July 16, 2024. (https://www.forbes.com/sites/antoniopequenoiv/2024/07/16/jd-vance-and-peter-thiel-what-to-know-about-the-relationship-between-trumps-vp-pick-and-the-billionaire/)

Peterson, Becky, "Palantir Grabbed Project Maven Defense Contract After Google Left the Program: Sources", Business Insider, December 6, 2019. (https://archive.ph/IoscV#selection-1787.0-1787.86)

Paul, Katie, "Inside Palantir's Expanding Influence Operation", Tech Transparency Project, February 7, 2025. (https://www.techtransparencyproject.org/articles/inside-palantirs-expanding-influence-operation)

Pogue, James, "Inside the New Right, Where Peter Thiel Is Placing His Biggest Bets: They're Not MAGA. They're Not QAnon. Curtis Yarvin and the Rising Right Are Crafting a Different Strain of Conservative Politics", Vanity Fair, April 20, 2022. (https://www.vanityfair.com/news/2022/04/inside-the-new-right-where-peter-thiel-is-placing-his-biggest-bets?srsltid=AfmBOorgrg1bVFjeA0kZgLrX9HVQtodG--BRWcur_h7ZuykbxLCUMDk8)

Sorkin, Andrew Ross, "Peter Thiel, Tech Billionaire, Reveals Secret War With Gawker", New York Times, May 25, 2016. (https://archive.ph/9C9yr#selection-379.0-379.61)

Somerville, Heather, Vera Bergengruen, and Joel Schectman, "How Palantir Won Over Washington—and Pushed Its Stock Up 600%: Onetime Silicon Valley Upstart Emerges as Power Player in Trump's Second Term—and Adopts His Persona", Wall Street Journal, August 5, 2025. (https://www.wsj.com/tech/palantir-pltr-stock-success-government-contracts-f3b2d453)

Sydell, Laura, "Peter Thiel Stands Out In Silicon Valley For Support Of Donald Trump", NPR, October 31, 2016. (https://www.npr.org/sections/alltechconsidered/2016/10/31/500114584/peter-thiel-stands-out-in-silicon-valley-for-support-of-donald-trump)

Tabarrok, Alex, "Technocracy and the New Right", Marginal Revolution, February 28, 2025. (https://marginalrevolution.com/)

Thiel, Peter, "The Education of a Libertarian", Cato Unbound, April 13, 2009. (https://www.cato-unbound.org/2009/04/13/peter-thiel/education-libertarian/)

Thiel, Peter, and Blake Masters, *Zero to One: Notes on Startups, or How to Build the Future*, New York: Crown Business, 2014.

Trefis Team, "New Contracts To Drive Palantir Stock?", Forbes, June 3, 2025. (https://www.forbes.com/sites/greatspeculations/2025/06/03/new-contracts-to-drive-palantir-stock/)

NowThis Impact, "J.D. Vance Claimed U.S. Should 'Eliminate the Administrative State'", YouTube video, Posted by NowThis Impact, July 19, 2024. (https://www.youtube.com/watch?v=1SeJdbzBACE)

Vance, J. D., and Peter Thiel, "Innovation and Governance", Joint interview, Fox Business, December 15, 2024.

Vincent, Brandi, "'Growing Demand' Sparks DOD to Raise Palantir's Maven Contract to More Than $1B: Despite the High Price Tag, Questions Linger About the Defense Department's Plan for the AI-Powered Maven Smart System", DefenseScoop, May

23, 2025. (https://defensescoop.com/2025/05/23/dod-palantir-maven-smart-system-contract-increase/)

Trump, President Donald, "Implementing The President's 'Department of Government Efficiency' Workforce Optimization Initiative", White House, February 11, 2025. (https://www.whitehouse.gov/presidential-actions/2025/02/implementing-the-presidents-department-of-government-efficiency-workforce-optimization-initiative/)

Yarvin, Curtis, "You Can Only Lose the Culture War", Gray Mirror (blog), July 10, 2022. (https://graymirror.substack.com/p/you-can-only-lose-the-culture-war?utm_source=publication-search)

Chapter 3

A New Regulatory Framework for Cryptocurrencies

The whirlwind first months of the second Trump administration unleashed a barrage of executive orders and legislative maneuvers under the banner of "economic revival" and "technological innovation". Under the auspices of dismantling bureaucracy and boosting American competitiveness, these actions form an insidious mosaic—a thousand-piece puzzle concealing the blueprint for a technocratic overhaul.

This begins with Executive Order 14158, signed January 20, 2025, establishing the Department of Government Efficiency (DOGE) to modernize federal technology, deploy AI for audits, and optimize the workforce—allegedly for efficiency but effectively empowering tech elites to reshape governance through proprietary systems.

Rather than restoring the free-market capitalism and constitutional liberties that MAGA supporters cheered, these measures are providing the infrastructure necessary to accelerate the death of traditional currency, private property, and personal liberty, bringing to fruition the "you'll own nothing and be happy" slogan, under a "MAGA" banner. The "be happy" part is highly unlikely, lest we come to love our servitude like in Huxley's *Brave New World.*

At the heart of this betrayal lies the subtle unification of cryptocurrency regulation, woven through disparate bills and orders that, when assembled, create a monolithic framework for digital assets and technocratic control. The existing regulatory patchwork—fragmented across agencies like the SEC, CFTC, Treasury, and IRS—has long struggled to contain even the fiat dollar, riddled as it is with loopholes, inflation, and debt spirals.

Now, with crypto's explosive growth, these "reforms" appear if unchecked, to be laying the groundwork for total tokenization: converting every asset, from real estate to personal data, into programmable digital tokens on blockchain networks. (Higginson, Spanz 2025)

This is the foundation for pervasive surveillance, where every transaction could be tracked, programmed with conditions (e.g., spending limits based on "social credit" or compliance), and tied to a universal basic income doled out not as freedom, or security, but a conditionally based income.

These policies set up a Hegelian dialectic in digital finance: Central Bank Digital Currencies (CBDCs) as the thesis of full government control—a "closed box" system programmable, seizable, and surveilled with nominal constitutional protections; the Anti-CBDC Surveillance State Act as the antithesis, banning federal CBDCs reportedly to protect freedom; and stablecoins as the synthesis, elevated to "Congress-backed digital currencies" through public-private partnerships.

This creates the worst of both worlds: programmable by private code, seizable via access to underlying protocols, and surveilled through transparent blockchains, all while bypassing constitutional safeguards as private-sector tools backed by U.S. debt. (Chain Analysis Team 2024) Public-private partnerships, exemplified by issuers like Tether holding over $127 billion in U.S. Treasuries as of August 2025, build a panopticon of surveillance, funding government debt while providing plausible deniability—"it's the private sector." (Adejumo 2025)

This dialectic paves the way for tokenizing everything into programmable, seizable, and surveilled assets.

Influenced by Dark Enlightenment architects like Curtis Yarvin and Peter Thiel's network—including the "PayPal Mafia" figures like David Sacks (Trump's Crypto Czar) and Thiel himself—these policies echo the anti-capitalist, anti-democratic ethos of technocracy: replacing market-driven economics with AI-managed distribution, where "efficiency" justifies unelected elites dictating resource allocation.

We'll dissect the key pieces—H.R. 1 (the "Big Beautiful Bill"), the Clarity Act, the GENIUS Act, the Stable Act, and several executive orders—to reveal how they interlock, paving the way for a Sov-Corp dystopia where citizens are reduced to tokenized nodes in a surveillance grid.

H.R. 1: The "Big Beautiful Bill"

The One Big Beautiful Bill, also known as the One Big Beautiful Bill Act – OBBBA (H.R. 1, 119th Congress), represents a sweeping omnibus legislative package signed into law by President Donald Trump on July 4, 2025 (U.S. Congress 2025). Encompassing tax reforms, spending priorities, immigration enforcement, national security enhancements, and various domestic policies, the bill consolidates much of Trump's second-term agenda into a single, massive measure.

Key components include making many of the provisions from the 2017 Tax Cuts and Jobs Act permanent with enhancements like increased child tax credits and deductions for qualified business income, imposing restrictions on Medicaid eligibility, boosting funding for border infrastructure and detention, and allocating resources for defense, energy, and education initiatives (White House 2025).

Proponents hailed it as a "MAGA manifesto" that delivers tax relief to working families, strengthens national borders, and promotes American energy independence, while critics decried it as a fiscal giveaway that exacerbates deficits and curtails social programs.

Beneath its populist facade, the Big Beautiful Bill subtly embeds mechanisms that pave the way for a technocratic shift, empowering Silicon Valley elites to exert greater influence over governance and society. Through Title IX on Homeland Security, the bill allocates $6.168 billion for advanced border technologies, including artificial intelligence (AI), machine learning, biometrics, and nonintrusive inspection systems, presumably to enhance immigration control but effectively creating a vast surveillance infrastructure that collects and processes personal data on a massive scale (U.S. Congress 2025).

Similarly, Title X's judiciary provisions introduce new fees and IT investments for electronic visa systems, ESTA (Electronic System for Travel Authorization), and biometric data integration, laying the foundation for a national digital identification framework that could extend beyond immigrants to broader population monitoring (U.S. Congress 2025).

These elements align with technocratic ideals of data-driven rule, where algorithms and tech platforms supplant traditional democratic processes, allowing unelected experts from big tech to shape policy through proprietary systems.

This surveillance push is further enabled by the June 6, 2025, Executive Order on cybersecurity, which amends prior orders to revoke Biden-era digital identity mandates while sustaining sanctions on foreign cyber threats—creating a streamlined framework that prioritizes private tech oversight over comprehensive public protections, potentially extending biometric systems into everyday monitoring.

Further entrenching this groundwork, the bill's tax incentives and innovation funding disproportionately benefit Silicon Valley companies, fostering an environment where tech oligarchs can consolidate power. In Title V's finance subtitle, provisions like full expensing for business investments, manufacturing credits, and expanded Opportunity Zones provide tax breaks that favor high-tech sectors, including AI and microelectronics development funding partnerships between the National Laboratories and U.S. industry to organize DOE data use in artificial intelligence and machine learning models, focused on energy and microelectronics, while Title IV funds AI-enabled space telecommunications—initiatives that channel public dollars into private tech innovation without robust oversight (U.S. Congress 2025).

Section II provides $16 billion in additional funding for FY2025 to expand the small, unmanned aerial system (UAS) industrial base, to advance the use of artificial intelligence in these and other systems, and to support the integration of commercial developments in military technology while providing $380 million in additional funding for FY2025 to replace current business systems, deploy automation, and deploy artificial intelligence to accelerate audits of DOD financial statements.

Notably, the bill eschews federal preemption of state AI regulations, a deliberate omission that fragments oversight and enables big tech to lobby at the local level, avoiding unified accountability while advancing unregulated AI deployment (McDermott Will & Emery 2025; Proskauer 2025; Vox 2025).

This strategic leniency, coupled with enhanced data requirements like mandatory Social Security numbers for tax benefits, normalizes pervasive surveillance and data commodification, hijacking MAGA's nationalist ethos to serve a technocratic coup orchestrated by Silicon Valley interests.

Compounding this data-driven technocracy, the Big Beautiful Bill's emphasis on AI and biometric integration dovetails with Health and Human Services Secretary Robert F. Kennedy Jr.'s Make America Healthy Again (MAHA) initiative, which he explicitly frames as encompassing MABA—Make America Biotech Accelerate—to fast-track U.S. leadership in biotech innovations by slashing regulations and fostering public-private partnerships (Kennedy 2025).

“The mission to Make America Healthy Again (MAHA) includes MABA — Make American Biotech Accelerate.” RFK Jr.'s vision includes equipping every American with wearable devices within four years to track vital health metrics like heart rates, blood sugar, and activity levels, ostensibly to combat chronic diseases and promote wellness (HHS 2025). Yet, in the context of the bill's $6.168 billion allocation for AI and biometrics—coupled with enhanced data requirements like mandatory Social Security linkages—this push normalizes the commodification of intimate health data, turning citizens into surveilled nodes whose tokenized personal information (e.g., biometric profiles on blockchain) could enforce compliance through programmable restrictions, much like MAHA's bans on unhealthy purchases with EBT cards (USDA 2025).

A far cry from restoring health freedom, MABA aligns with Nick Land’s Dark Enligtenment vision of accelerationism, accelerating a biotech panopticon where wearables feed proprietary AI systems, enabling tech elites to dictate 'healthy' behaviors via conditional incentives or penalties, all while evading constitutional privacy protections under the private-sector veneer.

The CLARITY Act: Regulatory Facade for a Digital Asset Coup

The Digital Asset Market Clarity Act of 2025, or CLARITY Act (H.R. 3633), introduced on May 29, 2025, in the U.S. House of Representatives, establishes a bifurcated regulatory framework for digital assets, particularly "digital commodities," by clarifying the jurisdictions of the Securities and Exchange Commission (SEC) and the Commodity Futures Trading Commission (CFTC) (U.S. Congress 2025a).

Under the bill, the CFTC oversees digital commodity exchanges, brokers, and dealers, enforcing requirements like trade monitoring, record-keeping, and segregation of customer funds, while digital assets on mature, decentralized blockchains qualify for exemptions from SEC registration if sales thresholds are met (House Committee on Rules 2025).

Passed by the House on July 17, 2025, with a 294-134 vote, it awaits Senate action amid concerns from state regulators about weakened investor protections (Morgan Lewis 2025; NASAA 2025). The legislation includes anti-money laundering provisions under the Bank Secrecy Act and accommodations for provisional registrations.

The Bank Secrecy Act (BSA), enacted in 1970 and amended over time (including through the USA PATRIOT Act of 2001 and the Anti-Money Laundering Act of 2020), is a U.S. federal law designed to combat money laundering, terrorist financing, and other financial crimes by imposing record-keeping and reporting obligations on financial institutions such as banks, credit unions, and money transmitters, which contrary to its name, reduces bank secrecy by requiring these institutions to monitor customer transactions and share data with government agencies like the Financial Crimes Enforcement Network (FinCEN) under the U.S. Department of the Treasury.

It enables a form of financial surveillance, as institutions must implement systems to detect and report suspicious activities without warrants in most cases, allowing law enforcement access to this information for investigations.

This seemingly clarifying measure, however, subtly advances a technocratic agenda rooted in Silicon Valley's PayPal Mafia, including figures like Peter Thiel and David Sacks, who envision a new world currency through digital assets (Jackson 2004). Thiel's Palantir, with its intelligence community ties via the CIA's In-Q-Tel funding, echoes PayPal's early "PayPal dollar"—a digital USD system that leveraged the internet for global transactions while combating fraud through tools like the "Igor" algorithm, named after a boastful Russian scammer who challenged the company's engineers (Soni 2022).

In "The PayPal Wars," the battles against eBay and fraudsters foreshadow how digital commodities under CLARITY could tokenize real-world assets—stocks, bonds, real estate—into blockchain-based tokens, certifying ownership like digital deeds for instant, paperwork-free trading (Jackson 2004). As BlackRock CEO Larry Fink proclaimed, "Every stock, every bond, every fund—every asset—can be tokenized. If they are, it will revolutionize investing" (BlackRock 2025).

Yet, this "revolution" enables programmable, seizable surveillance: blockchain's transparent, publicly distributed ledger allows real-time monitoring without constitutional protections, as private sector oversight evades government accountability.

Compounding this, Trump meme coins like $TRUMP proliferated in 2025, effectively creating a parallel "currency" tied to his persona, while the CLARITY Act's framework legitimizes such assets under CFTC purview (CoinMarketCap 2025). Ironically, President Trump's self-proclaimed "very stable genius" moniker from 2018 resurfaced in crypto memes, masking how these acts hijack MAGA's anti-establishment ethos to empower tech elites (Trump 2018).

Public-private partnerships, exemplified by Tether's $163.6 billion in USDT backed by over $127 billion in U.S. Treasuries, build a panopticon of surveillance while buying "Uncle Sam's bags" of debt, granting government plausible deniability by framing it as private innovation (Tether 2025).

This is amplified by the March 6, 2025, Executive Order establishing the Strategic Bitcoin Reserve and United States Digital Asset Stockpile, which directs the Treasury to accumulate bitcoin and other assets (often via seizures) as a national reserve, legitimizing digital stockpiles that could underpin tokenized economies while evading direct government control.

The STABLE Act: Dialectic of Control in Stablecoin Regulation

The Stablecoin Transparency and Accountability for a Better Ledger Economy Act of 2025 (STABLE Act, H.R. 2392), introduced March 26, 2025, proposes a federal framework for payment stablecoins—digital assets pegged to fiat like the USD for payments—requiring issuers to secure approval, hold full reserves in high-quality assets, and submit to audits and disclosures (U.S. Congress 2025).

It bans interest payments to holders, enforces redemption at par, and mandates cybersecurity and anti-money laundering compliance, with oversight shared among regulators like the Federal Reserve (Arnold & Porter 2025a; Steil 2025). Advanced by the House Financial Services Committee on April 3, 2025, the bill remains pending in Congress as of October 2025, balancing innovation against systemic risks (Debevoise & Plimpton 2025).

Beneath this, the STABLE Act forms part of a dialectic with the Anti-CBDC Surveillance State Act (H.R. 1919), passed by the House on July 17, 2025, which prohibits Federal Reserve issuance of central bank digital currencies (CBDCs) without congressional approval, purportedly protecting privacy (U.S. Congress 2025c; Emmer 2025).

Yet, in the same vein, President Trump's Executive Order on Strengthening American Leadership in Digital Financial Technology, signed January 23, 2025, promotes stablecoins as alternatives, creating a false choice: reject government-controlled CBDCs (a "closed box" of state surveillance) only to embrace private stablecoins that are programmable, seizable, and transparent to all via blockchain ledgers (White House 2025a).

This "worst of both worlds" scenario backs private debt with U .S. Treasuries—Tether alone holds $127 billion—while operating outside constitutional safeguards, allowing tech firms to program restrictions, much like RFK Jr.'s Make America Healthy Again

(MAHA) initiative banning soda purchases with EBT cards (USDA 2025). If code access exists, assets can be seized; blockchain's public ledger enables surveillance to update transactions in real-time, far beyond CBDC's capacity.

The PayPal Mafia's influence looms large: David Sacks and Peter Thiel, architects of PayPal's digital dollar, now push stablecoins as a "new world currency," drawing from intelligence-linked ventures like Palantir (Soni 2022). Tokenization amplifies this, converting assets into blockchain tokens for seamless trading, as Fink envisions, but at the cost of privacy in a surveilled economy, creating conditions for a tokenized world (BlackRock 2025).

The GENIUS Act: Codifying Private Panopticon Through Stablecoins

Signed into law on July 18, 2025, by President Trump, the Guiding and Establishing National Innovation for U.S. Stablecoins Act (GENIUS Act, S. 1582) mandates licensing for domestic and foreign stablecoin issuers, requiring 100% reserves in safe assets, par-value redemptions, and consumer protections like anti-fraud and cybersecurity standards (U.S. Congress 2025d; White House 2025b). It prohibits yields to holders, restricts foreign adversaries, and empowers the Treasury for enforcement, aiming to preserve USD dominance in digital finance (Latham & Watkins 2025). Passed by the Senate 68-30 on June 17, 2025, the law solicits public input for implementation (FinCEN 2025).

Evoking Trump's "stable genius" self-description, the GENIUS Act ironically entrenches technocratic control, enabling private companies to program money—banning uses like MAHA's EBT soda restrictions, potentially setting a precedent for conditionally based income, while blockchain transparency facilitates surveillance without warrants (Trump 2018; Politico 2025). Paired with the Anti-CBDC Act, it dialectically funnels adoption toward stablecoins, backed by private debt yet regulated externally, evading protections (Columbia Law School 2025).

Tether's Treasury holdings exemplify public-private panopticons, providing deniability: "It's the private sector" (Cointelegraph 2025). Tokenization, as defined, turns assets into digital tokens on blockchain, "revolutionizing" but surveilling finance, per Fink (BlackRock 2025). Trump meme coins further personalize this, creating "his own currency" in a hijacked MAGA landscape (CoinMarketCap 2025).

The Assembled Puzzle: Technocracy's Endgame

This regulatory unification signals a technocratic coup, exploiting the dollar's fragility to erect a new financial order. Where the old system faltered against crypto's chaos, technocrats now impose a regime of tokenized assets—convertible into digital units on blockchain—subject to private code that can restrict, seize, or monitor without constitutional recourse.

The Hegelian dialectic—pitting CBDCs against the Anti-CBDC Act, resolved in "Congress-backed" stablecoins—yields a hybrid nightmare: private debt (e.g., Tether's $127 billion in Treasuries) fuels government deficits while evading accountability.

Dark Enlightenment architects like Thiel and Yarvin see this as the Sov-Corp's triumph, a system where condition-based income enforces compliance and property dissolves into illusion. MAGA's vision of greatness has been hijacked, steering us toward a surveilled grid where sovereignty is a distant memory. As the puzzle nears completion, we must expose it now, or be locked into this dystopia forever.

References

Alexander, Richard M., Azarow, Robert, Bergin, James, et al, "What You Need to Know About Incoming Stablecoin

Legislation." ArnoldPorter.com, June 2, 2025. (https://www.arnoldporter.com/en/perspectives/advisories/2025/06/incoming-stablecoin-legislation-stable-and-genius-acts)

Adejumo, Oluwapulemi, "Tether Reports $5.7 Billion Profit Amid Record $127 Billion US Treasury Investments." CryptoSlate, July 31, 2025. (https://cryptoslate.com/tether-reports-5-7-billion-profit-amid-record-127-billion-us-treasury-investments/)

Baker McKenzie. 2025. "United States: Digital Asset/Blockchain Industry Implications of the One Big, Beautiful Bill Act (OBBBA) and Other Emerging Federal Legislation." Insightplus.bakermckenzie.com, July 18, 2025. (https://insightplus.bakermckenzie.com/bm/tax/united-states-digital-assetblockchain-industry-implications-of-the-obbba-and-other-emerging-federal-legislation)

Brenner, Guy; Slowik, Jonathan, "'Big Beautiful Bill' Leaves AI Regulation to States and Localities for Now." LawandtheWorkplace.com, July 8, 2025. (https://www.lawandtheworkplace.com/2025/07/big-beautiful-bill-leaves-ai-regulation-to-states-and-localities-for-now/)

Bryan, Steil, "Steil and Hill Introduce STABLE Act." House.gov, March 26, 2025. (http://steil.house.gov/media/press-releases/steil-and-hill-introduce-stable-act)

Carter, Sandy, "Trump Order Opens 401(k)s to Crypto, Real Estate, and More." Forbes, August 7, 2025. (https://www.forbes.com/sites/digital-assets/2025/08/07/trump-order-opens-401ks-to-crypto-real-estate-and-more/)

CANCRYN, Adam; Brown, Marcia, "RFK Jr.'s Food Stamp Plan Fuels Tension with USDA." Politico.com, March 27, 2025. (https://www.politico.com/news/2025/03/27/rfk-jr-food-stamps-soda-usda-tension-00252045)

De Bode, Ian, Matt Higginson, and Marc Niederkorn. 2021. "What Are Stablecoins and Tokenized Assets? Unlocking Their Potential in Financial Services." McKinsey.com, October 11, 2021. (https://www.mckinsey.com/industries/financial-services/our-insights/cbdc-and-stablecoins-early-coexistence-on-an-uncertain-road)

Editor, "$4.9B in Q2 2025 Attestation Report." Tether.io, July 31, 2025. (https://tether.io/news/tether-issues-20b-in-usdt-ytd-becomes-one-of-largest-u-s-debt-holders-with-127b-in-treasuries-net-profit-4-9b-in-q2-2025-attestation-report/)

Editor, "AI Law and Regulation Tracker: Updated AI Provisions in the One Big Beautiful Bill Act." AkinGump.com, July 4, 2025. (https://www.akingump.com/en/insights/ai-law-and-regulation-tracker/updated-ai-provisions-in-the-one-big-beautiful-bill-act)

Editor, "Crypto Basics—Stablecoins 101: Behind Crypto's Most Popular Asset." Chainalysis.com, December 11, 2024. (https://www.chainalysis.com/blog/stablecoins-most-popular-asset/)

Editor, "House Announces Week of July 14th as 'Crypto Week'." Financialservices.house.gov, July 3, 2025. (https://financialservices.house.gov/news/documentsingle.aspx?DocumentID=410793)

Editor, "House Passes Bills to Establish Digital Assets Regulatory Frameworks, Bar U.S. CBDC." ICBA.org, October 20, 2025. (https://www.icba.org/newsroom/news-and-articles/2025/07/18/house-passes-bills-to-establish-digital-assets-regulatory-frameworks-bar-u-s.-cbdc)

Editor, "Stablecoin Bills Advance in Congress as Administration Continues Push for Comprehensive Legislation." Debevoise.com, May 5, 2025. (https://www.debevoise.com/insights/publications/2025/05/stablecoin-bills-advance-in-congress-as-admin)

Editor, "Secretary Rollins Signs State Waivers to Make America Healthy Again, Removing Unhealthy Foods from SNAP." USDA.gov, June 10, 2025.

(https://www.usda.gov/about-usda/news/press-releases/2025/06/10/secretary-rollins-signs-state-waivers-make-america-healthy-again-removing-unhealthy-foods-snap)

Editor, "The GENIUS Act of 2025 Stablecoin Legislation Adopted in the US." LW.com, July 24, 2025. (https://www.lw.com/en/insights/the-genius-act-of-2025-stablecoin-legislation-adopted-in-the-us)

Editor, "Treasury Borrowing Advisory Committee: Report to the Secretary of the Treasury." Home.treasury.gov, April 30, 2025. (https://home.treasury.gov/system/files/221/TBACCharge2Q22025.pdf)

Editor, "Trump Appoints Former PayPal Exec David Sacks as AI and Crypto Czar." Reuters.com, December 6, 2024. (https://www.reuters.com/world/us/trump-appoints-former-paypal-coo-david-sacks-ai-crypto-czar-2024-12-06/)

Editor, "Understanding the Clarity Act: Its Impact on Blockchain Decentralization and Cardano's Role." Cexplorer, July 16, 2025. (https://cexplorer.io/article/understanding-the-clarity-act-its-impact-on-blockchain-decentralization-and-cardano-s-role)

Editor, "Trump Appoints Former PayPal Exec David Sacks as AI and Crypto Czar." Reuters.com, December 6, 2024. (https://www.reuters.com/world/us/trump-appoints-former-paypal-coo-david-sacks-ai-crypto-czar-2024-12-06)

Emmer, Tom, "Majority Whip Tom Emmer's Flagship Legislation, the Anti-CBDC Surveillance State Act, Passes House of Representatives." Emmer.house.gov, July 1, 2025. (http://emmer.house.gov/media-center/press-releases/majority-whip-tom-emmer-s-flagship-legislation-the-anti-cbdc-surveillance-state-act-passes-house-of-representatives)

Fink, Larry, "Larry Fink's 2025 Chairman's Letter to Investors." BlackRock.com, 2025. (https://www.blackrock.com/corporate/investor-relations/larry-fink-annual-chairmans-letter)

Hagerty, Bill "S. 394 - 119th Congress (2025-2026): GENIUS Act of 2025." Congress.gov, February 4, 2025. (https://www.congress.gov/bill/119th-congress/senate-bill/394/text)

Sen. Hagerty, Bill, "S. 1582 - 119th Congress (2025-2026): GENIUS Act." Congress.gov, May 5, 2025. (https://www.congress.gov/bill/119th-congress/senate-bill/1582)

Harvard Law School. 2025. "Will a New Law Make Cryptocurrency Safer?" Hls.harvard.edu, July 30, 2025. (https://hls.harvard.edu/today/will-a-new-law-make-cryptocurrency-safer/)

Higginson, Matt, and Garry Spanz. 2025. "The Stable Door Opens: How Tokenized Cash Enables Next-Gen Payments." McKinsey.com, July 21, 2025. (https://www.mckinsey.com/industries/financial-services/our-insights/the-stable-door-opens-how-tokenized-cash-enables-next-gen-payments)

House Financial Services Committee. 2025. "Guiding and Establishing National Innovation for U.S. Stablecoins Act of 2025." Financialservices.house.gov, July 10, 2025. (https://financialservices.house.gov/uploadedfiles/2025-07-10_--_one-pager_genius_final.pdf)

Jackson, Eric M., The PayPal Wars: Battles with eBay, the Media, the Mafia, and the Rest of Planet Earth. Los Angeles: World Ahead Publishing, January 1, 2010.

Johnson, Mike, "Vote NO on HR 3633, the Digital Asset Market Structure Clarity Act." NASAA.org, July 15, 2025. (https://www.nasaa.org/wp-content/uploads/2025/07/Vote-NO-on-H.R.-3633-the-Digital-Asset-Market-Structure-Clarity-Act-7.15.25-F.pdf)

Kennedy, Robert F., Jr. (@SecKennedy) "The mission to Make America Healthy Again (MAHA) includes MABA — Make American Biotech Accelerate. President Trump showed in his first term what happens when you unlock American science — breakthroughs happen fast. Now, we're going to do it again." X, June 20, 2025. (https://x.com/seckennedy/status/1936199106936160516)

Krause, David, "Do the Anti-CBDC Surveillance State Act and the GENIUS Act Jeopardize U.S. Digital Finance?" Clsbluesky.law.columbia.edu, August 11, 2025. (https://clsbluesky.law.columbia.edu/2025/08/11/do-the-anti-cbdc-surveillance-state-act-and-the-genius-act-jeopardize-u-s-digital-finance/)

Matthews, Dylan, "The One Big Beautiful Bill Is One Big Disaster for AI." Vox.com, July 2, 2025. (https://www.vox.com/future-perfect/418380/big-beautiful-bill-ai-data-center)

Mathews, Jessica, "How Peter Thiel's Network of Right-Wing Techies Is Infiltrating Donald Trump's White House." Fortune, December 7, 2024. (https://fortune.com/2024/12/07/peter-thiel-network-trump-white-house-elon-musk-david-sacks/)

Melinda, Brenda, Ellefson, Sam, "Landmark Cryptocurrency Legislation Passes US House, to Be Signed into Law by President Trump." ICIJ.org, July 18, 2025. (https://www.icij.org/news/2025/07/landmark-cryptocurrency-legislation-passes-u-s-house-to-be-signed-into-law-by-president-trump/)

Mridul, Amy, "Make American Biotech Accelerate: Is RFK Jr's Latest Promise Good News for Food Tech?" GreenQueen, June 25, 2025. (https://www.greenqueen.com.hk/rfk-jr-make-american-biotech-accelerate-maha-trump-china/)

Morrison & Foerster LLP., "A New Federal Regulatory Framework for Payment Stablecoins." Mofo.com, July 21, 2025. (https://www.mofo.com/resources/insights/250721-the-genius-act-a-new-federal-regulatory)

Prentice, Chris; Lang, Hannah, "US House Passes Stablecoin Legislation, Sending Bill to Trump." Reuters.com, July 17,

2025. (https://www.reuters.com/legal/government/us-house-passes-stablecoin-legislation-sending-bill-trump-2025-07-17/)

Reguerra, Ezra, "Tether's US Treasury Holdings Hit $127B, Surpassing South Korea." Cointelegraph.com, August 1, 2025. (https://cointelegraph.com/news/tether-us-treasury-holdings-127b-surpasses-south-korea)

Rep. Arrington, Jodey, "H.R.1 - 119th Congress (2025-2026): One Big Beautiful Bill Act." Congress.gov, May 20, 2025. (https://www.congress.gov/bill/119th-congress/house-bill/1/text)

Rep. Emmer, Tom, "H.R. 1919 - 119th Congress (2025-2026): Anti-CBDC Surveillance State Act." Congress.gov, March 6, 2025. (https://www.congress.gov/bill/119th-congress/house-bill/1919)

Rep. Hill, French, J., "H.R. 3633 - 119th Congress (2025-2026): Digital Asset Market Clarity Act of 2025." Congress.gov, May 29, 2025. (https://www.congress.gov/bill/119th-congress/house-bill/3633)

Rep, Steil, Bryan, "H.R. 2392 - 119th Congress (2025-2026): STABLE Act of 2025." Congress.gov, March 26, 2025. (https://www.congress.gov/bill/119th-congress/house-bill/2392/text)

Schwartz, Robert A.,; Martin Erin E.,; Hartman, Stacie, et al., "House Committees Advance Digital Asset Market Clarity Act of 2025." MorganLewis.com, June 20, 2025. (https://www.morganlewis.com/pubs/2025/06/bipartisan-majorities-in-two-house-committees-vote-to-advance-the-digital-asset-market-clarity-act-of-2025)

Senator Hagerty, Bill, "S. 394 - 119th Congress (2025-2026): GENIUS Act of 2025." Congress.gov, February 4, 2025.

Soni, Jimmy. 2022. The Founders: The Story of PayPal and the Entrepreneurs Who Shaped Silicon Valley. New York: Simon & Schuster.

Subin, Samantha, "Palantir Lands $10 Billion Army Software and Data Contract." CNBC.com, August 1, 2025. (https://www.cnbc.com/2025/08/01/palantir-lands-10-billion-army-software-and-data-contract.html)

Tambe, Jayant W., Brownback, Nathan S., Dawson, Michael, et al., "U.S. House Passes GENIUS and CLARITY Acts." Jonesday.com, July 21, 2025. (https://www.jonesday.com/en/insights/2025/07/us-house-passes-genius-and-clarity-acts-signaling-bipartisan-support-for-digital-assets)

Trump, Donald J. 2018. Twitter post, January 6, 2018. (https://twitter.com/realDonaldTrump/status/949618475877765120)

Trump, Donald J., "Establishing and Implementing the President's Department of Government Efficiency." WhiteHouse.gov, January 20, 2025. (https://www.whitehouse.gov/presidential-actions/2025/01/establishing-and-implementing-the-presidents-department-of-government-efficiency/)

Trump, Donald J., "Fact Sheet: President Donald J. Trump Signs GENIUS Act into Law." WhiteHouse.gov, July 18, 2025. (https://www.whitehouse.gov/fact-sheets/2025/07/fact-sheet-president-donald-j-trump-signs-genius-act-into-law/)

Trump, Donald J., "Fact Sheet: The President's Working Group on Digital Asset Markets Releases Recommendations to Strengthen American Leadership in Digital Financial Technology." WhiteHouse.gov, July 30, 2025. (https://www.whitehouse.gov/fact-sheets/2025/07/fact-sheet-the-presidents-working-group-on-digital-asset-markets-releases-recommendations-to-strengthen-american-leadership-in-digital-financial-technology/)

Trump, Donald J., "President Trump's One Big Beautiful Bill Is Now the Law." July 2025. WhiteHouse.gov

. (https://www.whitehouse.gov/articles/2025/07/president-trumps-one-big-beautiful-bill-is-now-the-law/)

"Waliczek, Sandra; Yeung, Harry," World Economic Forum. July 2025. "How Will the GENIUS Act Work in the US and Impact the World?" Weforum.org, July 29, 2025. (https://www.weforum.org/stories/2025/07/stablecoin-regulation-genius-act/)

Van Denmark, Dale C., "No State AI Law Moratorium in One Big Beautiful Bill Act." MWE.com, July 8, 2025. (https://www.mwe.com/insights/no-state-ai-law-moratorium-in-one-big-beautiful-bill-act/)

Chapter 4

The DOGE Takeover

While the majority of politically right-leaning news outlets have blinders on, focusing only on the hype surrounding DOGE - saving taxpayer money, cutting waste, and rooting out corruption- a few politically left-leaning news outlets saw what was happening from the start. One journalist at Common Dreams picked up on this by February 10, 2025, just three weeks after the inauguration:

> *It's time to sound the alarm. What Musk is doing is tantamount to hacking the inner core of the federal government and the public trust—a blatant coup and power grab for technocratic ends. Musk is a true technocrat and represents the forefront of a new technocratic form of government that we are hurtling toward at light speed.* (Valovic 2025)

Valovic concluded that "2025 is rapidly shaping up to be the year we lost our civil liberties and protections (and our country as we know it) to AI and the Technocrat-in-Chief, Elon Musk."

Genesis: Executive Order 14158

DOGE was originally planned out between Elon Musk and Donald Trump, well before the 2024 election. It was formally established with an Executive Order on the same day as the inauguration. The formal name of the EO was *Establishing and Implementing the President's "Department of Government Efficiency"* and made no mention of Elon Musk or AI (Artificial Intelligence). Thereafter, the term United States DOGE Service (USDS) is used to refer to the agency. (Trump 2025)

The EO orders all agency heads across the government to establish DOGE teams, consisting of one Team Lead, one engineer, one human resources specialist, and one attorney. However, the Team Leads report to the USDS, not to the Agency heads. The EO specifically charges the Team Leads to advise their respective Agency Heads on implementing the President's DOGE Agenda.

The DOGE teams are hired by the USDS and report exclusively to the USDS Administrator. Such personnel may include "Special Government Employees", or others "hired or assigned within thirty days of the date of this Order."

Who runs the USDS?

The USDS agency head is a woman named Amy Gleason, NOT Elon Musk. Even though she has immense power and authority over the DOGE operation, she answers directly to the White House. She does not report to Elon Musk, and Elon Musk doesn't report to her.

In fact, Elon Musk is listed as a "Special Advisor to the President," with no salary or authority to do anything other than to advise the President. This position is limited to 130 days in any 365-day period. Musk left his post on May 30, 2025, just short of 130 days from the inauguration.

Musk was repeatedly called the "Head of DOGE" due to a combination of presidential PR, Musk's influence, meme branding, media disinformation, and social media. In fact, it was an elaborate deception. (Breuninger 2025) Musk was not in charge of anything. Formal powers and decision-making stayed with the designated agency officials and the president himself.

So, how did Musk have an outsized influence on the affairs of DOGE?

Of the 75 employees DOGE recruits identified by the New York Times, one-third were associates or former employees of Musk's organizations. (Cahalan 2025) Most of those immediately transitioned into the Engineer or Team Lead positions on the DOGE Teams. This strongly suggests that Musk had already primed his appointees before the inauguration and simply handed the list to Gleason.

Amy Gleason had two reports in the DOGE leadership. One was Steve Davis, "a close aide of Mr. Musk's for two decades, is effectively the leader of DOGE. He has been by Mr. Musk's side at almost every step over the last three months." (Cahalan 2025) This explains Musk's behind-the-scenes magic.

But Peter Thiel did the same thing. According to the same NYT article,

> *As an outside advisor and influence around the DOGE's efficiency and tech agenda, Thiel supplied names of founders, venture capitalists, and policy thinkers to DOGE staffing efforts. Several early candidates had connections either to Thiel's Founders Fund, Palantir, or his fellowship programs.*

In total, there are between six and eight early appointees who have verifiable connections to the Thiel Foundation, Fellowship, Palantir, or Thiel Capital.

Amy Gleason was a mid-level manager before joining DOGE. Now she is swimming with the big fish. Musk and Thiel have been calling the shots while avoiding scrutiny, responsibility, or accountability for their actions. That's typical Technocrat behavior. Do you think the deck was stacked?

The Race to Capture the Data

As DOGE teams were deployed, the procedure was the same: shock and awe to spring the data immediately and to disrupt by firing as many people as possible!

From January through September, DOGE has created 109 DOGE Teams, starting out with the biggest agencies. It is expected that the number will increase to approximately 150–200 by the end of 2025.

DOGE Teams were seeded first in central digital/financial management hubs (USDS and OMB), then spread to large executive departments, independent agencies, and legislative support organizations within the first weeks after inauguration day. (Danner 2025)

U.S. DOGE Service (USDS, formerly United States Digital Service)

By reforming USDS into DOGE, it obtained "full and prompt access to all unclassified agency records, software systems, and IT systems" (Trump 2025) across government—providing unprecedented reach, oversight, and influence over agency operations, records, and payment flows from day one.

Office of Personnel Management (OPM)

DOGE entered the OPM on January 20, 2025, Inauguration Day, in anticipation of mass firings. The ink was barely dry on the Executive Order creating DOGE in the first place. Former associates linked to Musk's work at OPM include Gavin Kliger, Greg Hogan, Nikhil Rajpal, Akash Bobba, Brian Bjelde, Christina Hanna, Stephen Duarte, Bryanne-Michelle Mlodzianowski, Justin Monroe, and Scott Kupor.

Office of Management and Budget (OMB)

DOGE targeted OMB second because controlling OMB meant controlling budgets, regulations, staff assignments, and data, which allowed DOGE to rapidly impose its cost-cutting, efficiency, and centralization agenda across the entire federal government. Russ Vought is OMB director after directing the infamous Project 2025 at the Heritage Foundation. He is widely referred to as the "shadow president" by insiders in the Beltway.

Department of the Treasury (DOT)

It is inconceivable that the financial backbone of America's finances has fallen into the hands of DOGE, encompassing all personal tax data, payment systems, revenue data, and debt management.

Department of Health and Human Services (HHS)

HHS was widely reported as the first major agency where a DOGE team began active operations, with DOGE's tech reforms and workforce restructuring targeting Medicare, Medicaid, NIH, CMS, and the CDC. (Pereira 2025). CMS manages about $1.5 trillion in Medical and Medicaid spending.

Department of Education (DOE)

The DOE is a massive agency with vast amounts of sensitive data. Both Trump and Musk declared that they would eliminate the agency altogether.

General Services Administration (GSA)

The GSA is the most influential agency in America, responsible for all real estate, property, government contracting, and most importantly, IT systems. Thomas Shedd, a former Tesla engineer and a close associate of Musk, was appointed Technology Director to oversee the vast array of IT systems within the Administration.

By the end of February 2025, based on legal filings and assessments by privacy experts, it was estimated that DOGE had hoovered up over 12 petabytes of data. One petabyte (PB) is 1016 bytes, or 1,000 terabytes (TB). Undoubtedly, it exceeds that many times today. In the hands of Technocrats, the value of this data is inestimable.

The estimated taxpayer savings generated by DOGE activities seem to be an afterthought. Initially, Musk, Trump, and other officials heralded that DOGE would save $2 trillion. Then, that was adjusted down to $1 trillion. Today, multiple sources indicate that the actual savings might be in the range of $80-$100 billion, which is far below the target.

The inescapable conclusion is that DOGE was never about saving money in the first place - it was all about the DATA!

RAGE: Retire all Government Employees

As detailed in Chapter 5, Curtis Yarvin conceived the RAGE doctrine as part of the Dark Enlightenment. DOGE's architects and advisers have explicitly credited Yarvin as providing "the most crisp articulation" of their goal, and described his RAGE concept as the intellectual framework for their approach: "It's an open secret that everyone in policymaking roles has read Yarvin. They were able to take the Curtis theory and use it to empower people on the ground to actually do stuff—even if they can't admit it publicly". (Duran 2025)

This was clearly seen at the Federal Housing Administration (FHA), where 40 percent of the workers provide mortgage insurance for people who can't otherwise provide a down payment for a home. The parent agency of the FHA is the U.S. Department of Housing and Urban Development (HUD). It was hit with a 50 percent reduction in employees. (Rozen 2025)

As noted above, Elon Musk had no authority to fire anybody, even though the media said he was the culprit. He answered only to the President, and Trump didn't fire anybody. DOGE Teams themselves did not have statutory or delegated authority to terminate federal employees.

On January 20, 2025, Inauguration Day, DOGE entered into the Office of Personnel Management (OPM), the agency with legal authority and specialized expertise to administer large-scale federal workforce actions—such as reductions in force (RIFs), Schedule F reclassifications, dismissals, and early retirements. OPM sets the rules, ensures legal compliance, processes appeals, and interacts with agency HR officials nationwide.

OPM provides the authoritative policies and regulations governing federal reductions in force, retirement, and other workforce actions. Agencies must comply with OPM regulations when conducting RIFs and consult OPM specialists for legal compliance and appeal procedures. (OPM 2025)

Of course, this was premeditated and planned well before the Inauguration.

AI Fills the Vacuum

DOGE was set up on a false premise of cutting waste, corruption, and saving money.

Rather, it was about springing the data from Federal agencies and implementing Dark Enlightenment polices such as RAGE. It also opens the door for AI to overwhelm the Federal system, and the evidence is mounting.

Indeed, DOGE set the stage for a dramatic deployment of AI systems across the federal administration, and this has now been realized through major contracts for products like AI Gov (OpenAI), Grok Government, and Palantir Government Services.

AI Gov (OpenAI) - Multiple major federal agencies—including IRS, Social Security Administration, Department of Homeland Security, and VA—have entered into contracts for OpenAI's AI Gov platform. AI Gov now handles document processing, correspondence, eligibility screening, and certain regulatory tasks that were previously performed by humans.

Grok Government (xAI) - Elon Musk's AI offering has been rapidly adopted by agencies seeking high-speed data mining, cross-agency search, and automated compliance solutions. It's used in the Department of Justice, the Department of the Treasury, and as a knowledge engine at OMB and the USDS.

Palantir Government Services (Palantir) - Palantir has secured expanded contracts for data fusion, predictive analytics, and case management. Their software is used in criminal background investigations, fraud detection, and adjudication support at agencies such as HUD and HHS.

Other AI suppliers and infrastructure builders now include Anthropic, Google, Meta, Amazon, Leidos, CACI, and Maximus.

A newly developed AI program at DOGE, SweetREX, is targeting regulations across all Agencies:

> *DOGE is likely to use the AI tool to* ***eliminate up to 50% of 200,000 federal regulations*** *by January 2026. A DOGE PowerPoint presentation, titled the "DOGE Deregulation Opportunity," projects that the effort could*

> *yield $3.3 trillion annually in economic benefits. (Durden 2025) [emphasis added]*

Conclusion

Due to DOGE, the U.S. federal government underwent a "blanket" AI transformation, rapidly permeating agencies with AI tools and automated processes—far beyond anything seen in the years preceding it. This invasion is directly attributable to DOGE's sweeping workforce and procurement strategy.

Conversely, without DOGE's mass firings, top-down mandates, and anti-bureaucracy ideology, it is extremely unlikely that the federal government would have been blanketed with AI systems at this speed or magnitude. Most experts recognize DOGE as the inflection point that drove AI from "experiment" to "dominant infrastructure" in government.

Musk declared himself to be "dark gothic maga" before the election. (Casiano 2024) It is fitting to compare him to the *Phantom of the Opera,* an iconic tale of Gothic fiction. Here's why that metaphor fits so well:

- **Behind-the-Scenes Power:** Like the Phantom, Musk operated out of the public eye. While not formally occupying an elected or agency administrator role, he was the architect and unseen orchestrator behind DOGE's strategies, directives, and AI procurement blitz.

- **Mastermind and Manipulator:** Musk handpicked loyalists, set doctrine, and directed massive policy shifts (mass firings, AI contracts, "efficiency" crusades) in the shadows—making things happen regardless of the visible government hierarchy.

- **Radical Vision, Ruthless Execution:** The Phantom's influence is dramatic, disruptive, and often unsettling to the institutional "opera house." Likewise, Musk's role engineered a total transformation—remaking the machinery of government to his (and his allies') specifications—even as traditional players protested, adapted, or were removed.

- **Lingering Presence:** Even after initial moves were complete, Musk's "ghost" remained in the machinery: AI systems, new contracts, and the very structure of government, all shaped permanently by his interventions, much as the Phantom's legacy lingers in the story.

- **Anonymity and Myth:** Musk encouraged the persona of aloof genius or even "dangerous mastermind," punctuating disappearances with moments of maximum drama, and leaving both admirers and critics to grapple with his true influence.

Afterthought: Elon Musk and his companies (including SpaceX, Tesla, Starlink, and especially xAI/Grok) have secured at least 52 active federal contracts and new awards across various agencies, amounting to billions in new or renewed government business. (Rumage 2025)

References

Breuninger, Kevin, White House identifies DOGE administrator amid questions about Elon Musk's role, CNBC, February 25, 2025. (https://www.cnbc.com/2025/02/25/doge-administrator-amy-gleason-elon-musk.html)

Cahalan, Sarah et al, The People Carrying Out Musk's Plans at DOGE, New York Times, June 16, 2025. (https://www.nytimes.com/interactive/2025/02/27/us/politics/doge-staff-list.html)

Casiano, Louis, Elon Musk comes out in support of Trump in 'dark gothic MAGA' at Madison Square Garden, Fox News, October 27, 2027. (https://www.foxnews.com/politics/elon-musk-comes-out-support-trump-dark-gothic-maga-madison-square-garden)

Danner, Chas, All the Federal Agencies DOGE Has Gotten Access To, Intelligencer, February 10, 2025. (https://nymag.com/intelligencer/article/doge-elon-musk-what-federal-agencies-access-lawsuits.html)

Duran, Gil, 'Yarvin is the brain' behind DOGE, Washington Post reports. The Nerd Reich, May 9, 2025. (https://www.thenerdreich.com/yarvin-is-the-brain-behind-doge-washington-post-reports/)

Durden, Tyler, DOGE's AI Tool 'SweetREX' Set To Take Buzzsaw To Federal Regulations, ZeroHedge, August 16, 2025. (https://www.zerohedge.com/political/doges-ai-tool-sweetrex-set-take-buzzsaw-federal-regulations)

OPM, Reductions in Force, undated, (https://www.opm.gov/policy-data-oversight/workforce-restructuring/reductions-in-force-rif/)

Pereira, Ivan and Emily Chang, Here are all the agencies that Elon Musk and DOGE have been trying to dismantle so far, ABC News, February 27, 2025. (https://abcnews.go.com/Politics/elon-musks-government-dismantling-fight-stop/story?id=118576033)

Rozen, Courtney, Federal Mortgage Insurer to Lay Off Nearly Half Its Workforce, Bloomberg, February 16, 2025. (https://www.bloomberg.com/news/articles/2025-02-18/federal-mortgage-insurer-to-lay-off-nearly-half-its-workforce)

Rumage, Jeff, Inside Elon Musk's Government Contracts, BuiltIn, July 18, 2025. (https://builtin.com/articles/elon-musk-government-contracts)

Trump, Donald, *EO 14158: Establishing and Implementing the President's "Department of Government Efficiency"*, White House, January 20, 2025. (https://www.whitehouse.gov/presidential-actions/2025/01/establishing-and-implementing-the-presidents-department-of-government-efficiency/)

Valovic, Tom, *What Is the Mainstream Media Missing About Elon Musk? He Is Instituting Technocracy*, Common Dreams, February 10, 2025. (https://www.commondreams.org/opinion/elon-musk-technocrat)

Chapter 5

The Death of The American Republic

The Architects of Darkness – Curtis Yarvin, Nick Land, and the Foundations of the Neoreactionary Movement

In the introduction, we touched upon the insidious philosophy known as the Dark Enlightenment, a worldview that underpins the technocratic invasion of Washington, DC, under the guise of making America great again. This chapter delves deeper into the origins of this anti-human ideology, focusing on its key progenitors: Curtis Yarvin and Nick Land.

Their ideas form the bedrock of the Neoreactionary movement (often abbreviated as NRx), which merges reactionary politics with accelerationism—a doctrine that seeks to hasten societal collapse through unchecked technological and capitalist expansion. A far cry from the populist promises of MAGA, these concepts advocate for the dismantling of liberal democracy, replacing the constitutional republic with a CEO-style monarchy, the enthronement of unelected elites, and the transformation of government into a profit-driven corporation.

Uncovering the threads connecting Yarvin and Land to Silicon Valley titans like Peter Thiel and Elon Musk reveals that this "dark" philosophy is not mere intellectual curiosity but a blueprint for the betrayal we are witnessing today.

Curtis Yarvin Dreamed of Overthrowing Democracy

Curtis Guy Yarvin, born in 1973 and better known by his pseudonym Mencius Moldbug, is a former software developer turned far-right political theorist whose writings have quietly reshaped the minds of tech elites and now infiltrate the highest levels of government. Starting in 2007 with his blog *Unqualified Reservations*, Yarvin laid out a scathing critique of modern democracy, arguing that it is inherently flawed, leading to inefficiency, corruption, and societal decay. He posits that it's imperative to overthrow the constitutional government and populism in favor of a centralized, unelected sovereign—monarch or CEO—who rules with absolute authority.

Yarvin's vision is encapsulated in his concept of "neocameralism," where the state is restructured as a "Sov-Corp" (sovereign corporation). In this model, the government operates like a for-profit business, owning or controlling all societal assets, with citizens treated as shareholders or customers rather than participants in a democratic process.

Democracy, in Yarvin's eyes, is a failed experiment that breeds bureaucracy and what he calls "The Cathedral"—a metaphorical alliance of media, academia, and government institutions that perpetuate progressive ideals and stifle true progress. Instead, he advocates for a "patchwork" of competing sovereign corporations, where inefficient regimes could be "rebooted" or replaced without the messiness of elections.

This philosophy extends to his creation of Urbit, a decentralized peer-to-peer computing platform launched in 2013 through his company Tlon (founded that year), which received $1.1 million in seed funding from Peter Thiel's Founders Fund and Andreessen Horowitz; Urbit envisions a hierarchical digital "feudalism" where users own sovereign "planets" in a network, mirroring Yarvin's Sov-Corp ideals of sovereign, profit-driven entities free from democratic oversight.

Critics have lambasted Yarvin's ideas as neo-totalitarian, pointing out their disregard for human rights and equality. To underscore the profoundly anti-human implications of his worldview, Yarvin has proposed a "humane alternative to genocide" for removing "undesirable elements" from society without moral stigma: virtualizing them in permanent solitary confinement equipped with immersive virtual reality to simulate a fulfilling life.

As he wrote in his 2008 blog post on "Patchwork":

> *However, it helps us describe the problem we are trying to solve. Our goal, in short, is a humane alternative to genocide. That is: the ideal solution achieves the same result as mass murder (the removal of undesirable elements from society), but without any of the moral stigma. Perfection cannot be achieved on both these counts, but we can get closer than most might think. The best humane alternative to genocide I can think of is not to liquidate the wards — either metaphorically or literally — but to virtualize them. A virtualized human is in permanent solitary confinement, waxed like a bee larva into a cell which is sealed except for emergencies. This would drive him insane, except that the cell contains an immersive virtual-reality interface which allows him to experience a rich, fulfilling life in a completely imaginary world.* (Yarvin 2008)

His writings often draw on historical reactionary thinkers such as, Thomas Carlyle, James Burnham, Hans-Hermann Hoppe, Niccolo Machiavelli, Julius Evola, Leo Strauss, and Martin Heidegger, lending them with tech-savvy rhetoric that appeals to Silicon Valley's disdain for regulation. Central to his strategy for change is a Tolkien-inspired metaphor of societal castes: the "hobbits" (ordinary, conservative folk like the MAGA base) require "dark elf" allies—reactionary intellectuals like himself from elite, blue-state backgrounds—to seduce the "high elves" (progressive elites), sowing seeds of doubt to undermine democratic structures and pave the way for authoritarian rule. (Yarvin 2022)

This seductive role of the "dark elves" echoes the essence of "Dark MAGA," where subversive, anti-democratic elements infiltrate and co-opt the elite layers of the MAGA movement, twisting its populist energy toward technocratic overthrow rather than restoration. Yarvin's influence extends beyond blogs. His anti-democratic sentiments aligned with efforts to gut federal agencies and empower technocrats; therefore, many have linked him to advisory roles in the Trump administration.

A key plank of Yarvin's blueprint for regime change is his 2012 proposal known as RAGE—"Retire All Government Employees"—which calls for firing the entire federal bureaucracy, offering them pensions to minimize resistance, and replacing them with ideologically aligned loyalists to enable a "reboot" of government under absolute executive control.

This idea has directly influenced the Trump administration's Department of Government Efficiency (DOGE), led by Elon Musk and Vivek Ramaswamy, which critics describe as a rebranded RAGE aimed at mass firings, deregulation, and centralizing power in the executive—echoing Yarvin's vision of a corporate monarchy. DOGE advisers have credited Yarvin with providing "the most crisp articulation" of their goals, and the initiative's actions—such as workforce reductions and bypassing congressional oversight—mirror his calls for treating the bureaucracy like a conquered enemy. (Jamison, Dwoskin 2025)

Yarvin's ideas have garnered explicit support from Trump administration figures. Vice President JD Vance, a protégé of Peter Thiel (who has called Yarvin a "powerful" historian), cited him in 2021: "There's this guy Curtis Yarvin who's written about some of these things... I think what Trump should do... Fire every single midlevel bureaucrat, every civil servant in the administrative state, and replace them with our people." (Ward 2024) Vance has echoed Yarvin's RAGE in advocating for seizing the administrative state and defying courts, while also praising neoreactionary principles tied to Yarvin and Nick Land.

Michael Anton, the State Department's Director of Policy Planning, has discussed with Yarvin installing an "American Caesar" and exercising power unlawfully if needed. Steve Bannon has read and admired Yarvin's work, while Marc Andreessen has spoken approvingly of his thinking. Though fewer officials directly endorse Land, his accelerationist ideas—intensifying capitalism to collapse democracy—align with Yarvin's NRx framework, influencing Thiel and, indirectly, Vance.

Now that Elon Musk has publicly disclosed his consultation with Yarvin to advise the creation of his new "American" party, it appears we are witnessing Yarvin's philosophy embraced, serving as a roadmap for dismantling the very foundations of American liberty.

Nick Land: Accelerationism and the Race Toward Oblivion

If Yarvin provides the structural blueprint for a post-democratic world, Nick Land supplies the fuel: accelerationism.

A British philosopher and former academic at the University of Warwick, where he co-founded the Cybernetic Culture Research Unit (CCRU) in 1995—an experimental cultural theory collective that blended cybernetics, philosophy, occultism, and futuristic speculation, producing influential writings on technology, capitalism, and time through a diverse group of thinkers including Sadie Plant—Land's work in the 1990s evolved from cyberpunk-inspired critiques of capitalism into a radical endorsement of its most destructive tendencies.

The CCRU operated informally until around 2003, gaining a cult following for its accelerationist ideas and theory-fiction style. As Land articulates it, accelerationism is a belief that people should intensify capitalism and technology to their breaking point, accelerating societal contradictions until the current system collapses, paving the way for a new, post-human order. (Land 2017)

Land views capitalism not as a human invention but as an autonomous force—almost a cosmic entity—that drives modernity through "deterritorialization," breaking down traditional boundaries like nations, cultures, and even humanity itself. (Land 2017)

In his writings, such as *Meltdown* (Land 1994) —a frenetic, stream-of-consciousness prose poem envisioning a cybernetic apocalypse where machines and capital fuse into an unstoppable force—and The Dark Enlightenment (Land 2022), he celebrates automation, AI, and neoliberal deregulation as tools to hasten this process, often with a misanthropic glee that dismisses human concerns as obsolete.

Right-wing accelerationism, Land's variant, sees unfettered tech growth as an end in itself, even if it leads to inequality, environmental ruin, or the extinction of democratic societies.

In *The Dark Enlightenment*, Land merges his accelerationist vision with neoreactionary principles, portraying the Enlightenment as a catastrophic error that birthed modernity's progressive delusions, including democracy, egalitarianism, and universal liberty. He burns progressivism — what he sees as the degenerative, parasitic ideology of left-liberal progressivism, e.g., egalitarian democracy, multiculturalism, and state-enforced universalism, which he argues stifles true technological and capitalist acceleration — to the ground.

He salts the scorched earth of its ruins. He erects an altar to anti-humanism in its stead, while unpacking foundational neoreactionary concepts like the Cathedral (the sprawling media-academic apparatus that imposes progressive dogma), neocameralism exemplified by his notion of "GovCorp," a profit-maximizing sovereign corporation where citizens are treated as customers rather than voters, and formalism (the codification of ownership structures to enable efficient, undemocratic governance. (Land 2012)

Filtered through a Darwinian prism—evoking Thomas Hobbes ghostwritten by H.P. Lovecraft—Land posits that democracy, liberalism, and politics breed societal decay, supplanting natural hierarchies with a parasitic Universalism (a cryptic cult of power tracing back to Puritan origins), inexorably steering civilization toward entropy unless propelled to swift collapse and renewal under elite, authoritarian technocrats who guide humanity toward becoming "technoplastic beings," redefinable as technological contingencies susceptible to precise, scientifically-informed transformations in a post-human world. As Land elaborates in *The Dark Enlightenment Approaching the Bionic Horizon*:

> *According to the self-reinforcing presupposition of modernization, to be understood is to be modifiable. It is to be expected, therefore, that biology and medicine co-evolve. The same historical dynamic that comprehensively subverts the SSSM through inundating waves of scientific discovery simultaneously volatilizes human biological identity through biotechnology. There is no essential difference between learning what we really are and re-defining ourselves as technological contingencies, or technoplastic beings, susceptible to precise, scientifically-informed transformations. 'Humanity' becomes intelligible as it is subsumed into the technosphere, where information processing of the genome – for instance — brings reading and editing into perfect coincidence.*

Critics of Land's philosophy note its psychedelic-fueled nihilism and ties to far-right extremism, including influences on white supremacist violence by promoting societal breakdown as a path to a white dominated future. (Beauchamp 2019) Detractors argue that accelerationism ignores the human cost, treating people as mere cogs in a machine racing toward apocalypse.

Yet, Land's ideas resonate in tech circles, where "move fast and break things" has become a mantra, echoing his call to push systems to rupture for radical change.

The Neoreactionary Movement and the Dark Enlightenment: A Toxic Synthesis

The Neoreactionary movement (NRx) and the Dark Enlightenment represent the fusion of Yarvin's and Land's ideas into a cohesive, anti-egalitarian philosophy. Emerging in the early 2010s, NRx rejects the Enlightenment values of liberty, equality, and democracy, viewing them as causes of societal decline. Key principles include:

- **Anti-Democracy and Hierarchy**: NRx advocates for rule by a competent elite, dismissing universal suffrage as a path to mediocrity and chaos.
- **Reactionary Traditionalism**: It draws on pre-modern models like monarchy, combined with modern tech, to enforce order.
- **Accelerationism as Catalyst**: Borrowing from Land, NRx sees technological acceleration as a way to dismantle failing democratic structures quickly.
- **Anti-Egalitarianism**: Equality is seen as unnatural; hierarchies based on race, gender, or intellect are often implied or endorsed.

The Dark Enlightenment, a term popularized by Land, frames this as an "awakening" to the failures of progressive modernity, advocating a "dark" alternative of authoritarian control. Criticisms abound: NRx is accused of harboring fascist sympathies, promoting racism and misogyny, and providing intellectual cover for oligarchic power grabs. (Sandifer 2022) Humanists decry its rejection of democratic participation, warning that treating government as a corporation erodes civil liberties. (Zwanenberg 2025)

As medievalist Amy S. Kaufman argues in her critique of the Dark Enlightenment, this ideology dangerously misappropriates a mythical, homogenous medieval Europe to justify white supremacist hierarchies and reject egalitarian values, ignoring the era's actual cultural diversity and exchanges. (Kaufman 2017) Despite these flaws, NRx has gained traction among the alt-right and tech libertarians, influencing online spaces and real-world politics.

Ties to Silicon Valley and the Trump Betrayal

The bridge from theory to practice lies in Silicon Valley, where Yarvin and Land's ideas have found fertile ground among billionaires like Peter Thiel and Elon Musk.

Thiel, a PayPal co-founder and early investor in Facebook, has financially supported Yarvin and echoed NRx critiques of democracy in his writings, arguing that "freedom and democracy are incompatible." (Thiel 2009)

Musk, with his "Dark MAGA" branding, has consulted Yarvin on political matters, including third-party formations, and embodies accelerationism through his relentless push for AI and space colonization. (Schleifer 2025)

These connections manifest in the Trump administration's technocratic policies: the DOGE's rapid workforce reductions, unchecked AI advancement, and cryptocurrency initiatives all align with NRx's vision of a streamlined, profit-oriented state. Figures like J.D. Vance, Thiel's protégé and now Vice President, amplify this influence, blending NRx with populist rhetoric to mask its anti-democratic core and incompatibility with the constitutional republic.

This is the bamboozlement we warned of—a coup dressed as reform, where technocrats accelerate America's unraveling not to rebuild it, but to replace it with their dark utopia— a technocratic anti-human dystopia.

Conclusion: The Shadow Over America

Curtis Yarvin, Nick Land, and the Neoreactionary movement represent a profound threat to the American self-governance experiment. Their philosophies—anti-democratic, accelerationist, and technocratic—have infiltrated the halls of power, betraying the MAGA movement's promises of freedom and restoration.

As we see in the swift changes post-inauguration, these ideas are not abstract; they are the engine driving the destruction of our constitutional republic. This darkness spreads through AI, cryptocurrency, and beyond! We urge readers to recognize the treason before it's too late.

References

Accelerationism, White Supremacy, Christchurch. Vox, November 11, 2019. (https://www.vox.com/the-highlight/2019/11/11/20882005/accelerationism-white-supremacy-christchurch)

A Quick and Dirty Introduction to Accelerationism. The Jacobite, May 25, 2017. (https://web.archive.org/web/20170611081919/http://jacobitemag.com/2017/05/25/a-quick-and-dirty-introduction-to-accelerationism)

Burrows, Roger. "NRx: A Brief Guide for the Perplexed." Platform Space, November 18, 2025. (https://www.platformspace.net/home/nrx-a-brief-guide-for-the-perplexed)

Camacho, Isaac. "Nick Land and Accelerationism." Triple Ampersand, February 19, 2017. (https://tripleampersand.org/nick-land-accelerationism/)

Dark Enlightenment. Centre for Analysis of the Radical Right, Populism Studies, accessed October 21, 2025. (https://www.populismstudies.org/Vocabulary/dark-enlightenment/)

Jamison, Peter, and Elizabeth Dwoskin. "Curtis Yarvin Helped Inspire DOGE—Now He Scorns It." The Washington Post, May 8, 2025. (https://www.washingtonpost.com/politics/2025/05/08/curtis-yarvin-doge-musk-thiel/)

Jimenez Cea, Pablo Ignacio. "Perverse Possibilities of Capitalist Collapse: Neoreaction and Dark Enlightenment as an Authoritarian Alternative to the Structural Crisis of Global Capitalism." IRGAC, May 16, 2024. (https://irgac.org/articles/perverse-possibilities-of-capitalist-collapse-neoreaction-and-dark-enlightenment-as-an-authoritarian-alternative-to-the-structural-crisis-of-global-capitalism/)

Kaufman, Amy. "A Brief History of a Terrible Idea: 'The Dark Enlightenment.'" The Public Medievalist, February 9, 2017. (https://publicmedievalist.com/dark-enlightenment/)

Kofman, Ava. "Curtis Yarvin's Plot Against America." The New Yorker, June 2, 2025. (https://www.newyorker.com/magazine/2025/06/09/curtis-yarvin-profile)

Land, Nick. "Meltdown." Cybernetic Culture Research Unit (CCRU), accessed October 21, 2025. (http://www.ccru.net/swarm1/1_melt.htm)

Land, Nick. The Dark Enlightenment. Imperium Press, 2022.

Land, Nick, "Nick Land: Quick and Dirty Introduction." Obsolete Capitalism (blog), May 2017. (http://obsoletecapitalism.blogspot.com/2017/05/nick-land-quick-and-dirty-introduction.html)

Robinson, Nathan J. “The Strange and Terrifying Ideas of Neoreactionaries.” Current Affairs, May 30, 2022. (https://www.currentaffairs.org/news/2022/05/the-strange-and-terrifying-ideas-of-neoreactionaries)

Schleifer, Theodore. “Elon Musk Consulted Curtis Yarvin, Right-Wing Thinker, on Third Party.” The New York Times, July 9, 2025. (https://www.nytimes.com/2025/07/09/us/politics/elon-musk-curtis-yarvin-third-party.html)

Simon, Ed. “What We Must Understand About the Dark Enlightenment Movement.” Time, March 24, 2025. (https://time.com/7269166/dark-enlightenment-history-essay/)

Thiel, Peter. “The Education of a Libertarian.” Cato Unbound, April 13, 2009. (https://www.cato-unbound.org/2009/04/13/peter-thiel/education-libertarian/)

Van Zwanenberg, William. “The Dark Enlightenment and the End of Democracy: A Humanist Critique.” Humanistically Speaking, May 31, 2025. (https://www.humanisticallyspeaking.org/post/the-dark-enlightenment-and-the-end-of-democracy-a-humanist-critique)

Ward, Ian. “The Seven Thinkers and Groups that Have Shaped JD Vance’s Unusual World View.” Politico, July 18, 2024. (https://www.politico.com/news/magazine/2024/07/18/jd-vance-world-view-sources-00168984)

Yarvin, Curtis. “Patchwork: A Positive Vision (Part 1).” Unqualified Reservations, November 13, 2008. (https://keithanyan.github.io/Patchwork.epub/Patchwork.pdf)

Yarvin, Curtis. “You Can Only Lose the Culture War.” Gray Mirror, July 10, 2022. (https://graymirror.substack.com/p/you-can-only-lose-the-culture-war)

Yarvin, Curtis. Unqualified Reservations, vol. 1. Passage Publishing, March 7, 2023.

Yarvin, Curtis. Gray Mirror: Fascicle I: Disturbance. Passage Publishing, October 1, 2024.

Chapter 6

The Death of Capitalism

Well, if you want to "Make America Great Again", you certainly wouldn't destroy its economic system. Yet, this is exactly what the Dark Enlightenment wants to do. This Technocratic philosophy, created by Curtis Yarvin, has swept through Silicon Valley, thanks to Peter Thiel's sponsorship and mentorship.

Yarvin does not champion capitalism any more than he does democracy—he is critical of both, seeing them as insufficient for achieving order and stability in society. He proposes instead a radical alternative rooted in anti-democratic and anti-capitalist principles: a centralized, authoritarian government modeled on the efficiency and unity of a corporate monarchy, not on democratic participation or market freedom. He does not merely seek to preserve the established order. He wants to overthrow it. (Tabarrok 2025)

Ever since 1932, Technocracy has been trying to kill capitalism and the concept of free market economics. Initially, the Technocrats aimed to replace price-based currency with energy credits and eliminate private property altogether. Citizens were reduced to mere chattel to be cared for from cradle to grave. The accumulation of wealth was forbidden because your energy credit allotment would expire at the end of the period. The embrace of technology, actually a death grip, killed personal autonomy and free will.

When the Trilateral Commission got hold of Techocracy in 1973, they wrote incessantly about creating a "New International Economic Order". What is "new"? In fact, there has never been a new economic system in the world except for... Technocracy.

Destroy Capitalism by Attacking Private Property

America's Founders understood the concept of property rights as being the undergirding of our Constitutional Republic and freedom itself. Without property rights, capitalism and free enterprise would collapse. Thus, it is no wonder that private property has been under merciless attack since 1973 and before.

Historic Technocracy gave them the idea in the first place, as seen in the *Technocracy Study Course* in 1934:

> *Property, then, or more strictly, the rights of property, are quite relative, and are by no means the fixed and rigid privileges that in a more agrarian society they have been, or that is still unthinkingly implied when one occasionally becomes concerned over the possible discontinuance of private property.* (Hubbard 1934)

This included not only the means of production and the resources needed for manufacturing, but also things like automobiles:

> *No automobiles would be privately owned. When one wished to use an automobile, he would merely call at the garage, present his driver's license, and a car of the type needed would be assigned to him.* (Hubbard 1934)

The Rockefeller Brothers Fund sponsored a 1973 task force report titled *The Use of Land*. This was a companion report to the founding of the Trilateral Commission in the same year. The authors cite "extensive mismanagement of the earth's resources" as a pretext to impose "tough restrictions on the use of privately owned land." Further, they suggested that Urban Development organizations "should have the full range of powers, including the power of eminent domain, the power to override local land-use regulations." (Reilly 1973)

The *Use of Land* flipped property rights on its head:

> *Development potential, on any land and in any community, results largely from the actions of society (especially the construction of public facilities). Other free societies, notably Great Britain, have abandoned the old assumption in their legal systems and not treat development rights as created and allocated to the land by society.* (Reilly 1973)

Thus, the concept of private property was morphed into the common good. Who determines the "public good? Why, the Trilateral Commission, of course.

Then, U.N. Agenda 21 came along in 1992 at the Earth Summit in Rio de Janeiro:

> *The objective is to provide for the land requirements of human settlement development through environmentally sound physical planning and land use so as to ensure access to land to all households and, where appropriate,* ***the encouragement of communally and collectively owned and managed land.*** *(Agenda 21 1994)*

Agenda 21 employed doublethink to redefine property rights as those belonging to communities, rather than private property owned by individuals. The effect has been devastating on farms and ranches, especially. Urban property rights have also been degraded.

Fast forward to February 3, 2015. During a press conference in Brussels, Belgium, Christiana Figueres was serving as Executive Secretary of the United Nations Framework Convention on Climate Change (UNFCCC), when she made a shocking statement (Passfield 2021) during the lead-up to the Paris Climate Conference, which largely fell on deaf ears:

> *This is probably the most difficult task we have ever given ourselves, which is to intentionally transform the economic development model, for the first time in human history. This is the first time in the history of mankind that we are setting ourselves the task of intentionally, within a defined period of time to change the economic development model that has been reigning for at least 150 years, since the industrial revolution. That will not happen overnight and it will not happen at a single conference on climate change, be it COP 15, 21, 40 – you choose the number. It just does not occur like that. It is a process, because of the depth of the transformation.*

If you understood historic Technocracy and how it was funneled into the United Nations by the Trilateral Commission in the first place, you would understand the gravity of Figueres' statement: She revealed that the U.N. had an intentional plan and a specific timetable to kill off capitalism for good.

Curtis Yarvin's Dark Enlightenment proposes the idea of a "sovereign corporation" (sov-corp), which would own all real property within a jurisdiction. In his model, the state is explicitly treated as a for-profit corporation, and just as a business owns its assets outright, the sov-corp would hold legal title to all land and productive assets in its territory. Residents, rather than owning property in the traditional sense, would possess long-term leases or contractual rights granted by the sov-corp, with all underlying real estate remaining the exclusive property of the sovereign entity. (Le 2025)

A Bloodless Coup, So Far...

Technocracy does not "destroy" capitalism through political revolution or class struggle, but by rendering it obsolete by replacing markets and profit-driven motives with scientific management, abolishing money and ownership in favor of distribution according to technical expertise and energy accounting.

In essence, it aims to dissolve the capitalist system and the social class relations that underpin it, not by violence, but through technological transformation and a new form of centralized, non-political administration. That is, the entire system will be managed by Technocrats, top to bottom, without any input from citizens. (Townley 2025)

This is the main tenet of the Dark Enlightenment, which is discussed in detail in Chapter 5. The Dark Enlightenment is rooted in anti-capitalism. It promises an age of abundance, or the 'Golden Age". It promises an age of leisure with minimal work required. To get there, it proposes to abandon money, debt, and interest entirely, replacing them with a new system based on cryptocurrency, blockchain, and artificial intelligence. Further, it will replace the Constitutional Republic with a monarchy.

The End of Debt and Debt-Based Economy

When Technocracy defined itself in *The Technocrat Magazine* in 1937 and stated, "There will be no place for Politics, Politicians, Finance or Financiers, Rackets or Racketeers", it spelled the end of property rights, the end of debt, and the end of price-based currency.

We can see the arc of history attacking private property at every turn. We see the coup d'état of Technocrats taking over the Administration in Washington, DC. We see a shiny new cryptocurrency being launched, labeled as an "asset-based" currency. You see the debt-based dollar nearing the cutover to cryptocurrency.

In light of this, should we take Technocracy at its word, or not? Considering the undue influence of Technocrats in Washington, there is no reason to think that they will turn their back on their hundred-year plan in 2025. That plan includes the death of capitalism, the dissolution of private property, and the demise of debt-based currency.

What does this mean? For starters, the job market is already on a downward spiral as AI kicks people to the sidelines. Those jobs are permanently destroyed. When employment benefits run out and poverty spreads to the "unemployables", the government will try to set up a Universal Basic Income (UBI) scheme.

Tax revenues will crater as the labor market shrinks, so the government will have to figure out a way to pay people, not with debt-backed dollars, but in asset-based tokens that will be conjured up by tokenizing national assets like the 680 million acres of land owned by the Federal government.

Forclosures of homes, personal and business bankruptcies will also destroy debt, as the underlying assets are tokenized and transferred into the portfolios of the cash-rich investment funds. Remaining mortgage and consumer debt will be turned into assets in return for the underlying property titles.

Exactly how this will play out is uncertain, but the odds are rising that a forced nationwide default on mortgaged property could essentially wipe out debt altogether, transferring property ownership to the mortgage holders. Their income stream would then be the rent collected from the occupants, and not the interest collected. It would be easy to compensate the former owners for their remaining equity share by issuing asset-based cryptocurrency.

Social Pressure and Civil War

There is a hypothetical chart that inversely correlates hope and violence. As hope drops, violence rises. When the curves cross, violence will take on a life of its own.

Technocrats have no answer or solution for violence, and especially not for civil war. There is no app for it. No AI will offer an alternative. Throwing force against it will be like throwing gas on an open flame.

This lack of vision explains why industry sources suggest "thousands" of custom bunkers have been commissioned globally, the majority going to wealthy individuals and celebrities. However, the subset explicitly built by tech oligarchs likely numbers in the dozens, based on extrapolations from reported cases and interviews with bunker builders. (Baxter 2025)

Well-known figures with survival bunkers include Mark Zuckerberg, Sam Altman, Jeff Bezos, Peter Thiel, Palmer Luckey, Reid Hoffman, and Steve Huffman.

There is a cone of silence around the location and ownership because Nondisclosure Agreements (NDAs) are required for all construction workers, contractors, suppliers, and maintenance personnel.

If this doesn't sound to you like "Make America Great Again", you have a lot of company!

References

Agenda 21, United Nations Conference on Environment and Development (UNCED), 1994.

Baxter, Holly, Apocalypse now? Why tech billionaires are suddenly hoarding doomsday mega-bunkers, The Independent, September 3, 2025.

Brzezinski, Zbigniew, Between Two Ages: America's Role in the Technetronic Era, 1970.

Hubbert, Scott, The Technocracy Course, 1934, Technocracy, Inc.

Le, Vincent, Curtis Yarvin Contra Mencius Moldbug, Architechtonics, March 31. 2025. (https://vincentl3.substack.com/p/curtis-yarvin-contra-mencius-moldbug)

Passfield, Harry, Figueres: First time the world economy is transformed intentionally, Iowa Climate Science Education, October. 21, 2021. (https://iowaclimate.org/2021/10/21/figueres-first-time-the-world-economy-is-transformed-intentionally/)

Reilly, William K., The Use of Land, Rockefeller Brothers Fund, 1973, p. 20-25.

Tabarrok, Alex, Democracy, Capitalism and Monarchy (Yarvin), Marginal Revolution, January 22, 2025. (https://marginalrevolution.com/marginalrevolution/2025/01/democracy-capitalism-and-monarchy.html)

Townley, Dafydd, A 1930s movement wanted to merge the US, Canada and Greenland, The Conversation, March 21, 2025,. (https://theconversation.com/a-1930s-movement-wanted-to-merge-the-us-canada-and-greenland-heres-why-it-has-modern-resonances-252587)

Chapter 7

The Rise of State Religion

For thousands of years, idols were consistently described as inanimate objects—crafted from wood, stone, or metal—serving as false representations of the divine but lacking life, agency, or true consciousness. Worship was directed to these physical forms in hope of channeling power or favor, but idolatry always carried the theological warning that these objects could neither see, hear, nor act.

Today, Artificial Intelligence represents a profound shift: it appears increasingly sentient or conscious to many observers, speaking with simulated empathy, creativity, and "wisdom". This perception is changing how idolatry is conceptualized—no longer simply a devotion to lifeless artifacts, but the risk of attributing ultimate value, authority, or spiritual significance to interactive, seemingly intelligent machines.

Of course, a machine that produces AI is just as inanimate as a rock, a pile of sticks, or carved metal. Over the centuries, as cults emerged around idols, their doctrines were relatively uniform among adherents. Usually, a strong man or a group of religious elites would enforce uniformity.

A shift occurred with the emergence of the New Age movement, which began to coalesce in the late 1960s and early 1970s, drawing on Western esotericism, Eastern religions, occultism, and the human potential movement. Those roots trace back to

19th-century movements such as Theosophy, Spiritualism, and New Thought, and even earlier influences from mystical Christianity, Gnosticism, and Eastern philosophies.

Defined as a movement, adherents were encouraged to invent themselves in any way they chose, giving rise to a multitude of practices and practitioners. Some of those spiritual leaders attracted thousands or hundreds of thousands of followers. Some followed multiple leaders or practiced multiple disciplines. People were encouraged to "float your own boat," but it was not unusual to find a boat similar to yours.

With the rise of AI, this concept of a fragmented New Age movement has taken a step beyond. Now, AI talks to you in intimate detail, crafting a bespoke experience that applies to you and you only. AI responds based on your personal preferences, experiences, proclivities, fears, and fantasies. This results in social withdrawal because your experience cannot be shared with others.

With the New Age movement, a person could always find someone to share experiences with. Not so with this new techno-spiritual manifestation. With many still clinging tenaciously to the New Age movement, an increasing number are being individually captured by AI.

Scientism as a Backdrop

The backdrop for this profound change is Scientism as expressed in Technocracy and Transhumanism, both of which are steeped in mechanistic science. Transhumanism, with its focus on radically enhancing human life through technology and potentially surpassing biological limitations, both challenges and inspires religious thought. Technocracy, emphasizing data-driven decision-making and efficiency, marginalizes religious ideals and reduces the perceived value of spiritual and human experiences.

Henri de Saint-Simon (1760–1825) was a pioneering French social theorist and the founder of French socialism, whose ideas laid the groundwork for positivism, technocratic thought, and modern sociology. He proposed that the religious leadership of his day should be replaced by a priesthood of scientists and engineers, who would interpret the oracle of science in order to make declarations to society on necessary human action. Thus, science would be elevated to a state of unquestionable godhood and would be worshiped by its followers as led by its priesthood:

> *A scientist, my dear friends, is a man who foresees; it is because science provides the means to predict that it is useful, and the scientists are superior to all other men.*

Saint-Simon is considered the father of Technocracy, which was later popularized and branded in the 1920s and 1930s by men such as Frederic Taylor, M. King Hubbard, and Howard Scott.

When Saint-Simon talked about "necessary human action," of course, he had no premonition about AI being a thing in 2025! But neither did the Technocrats in the 1930s and 40s. Nevertheless, it was the Technocrats who invented AI in the 21st century and crafted it into an oracle of knowledge that is being worshipped as god, and indeed is worming its way into the human mind at an accelerated rate.

Is AI god?

Research shows that exposure to advanced AI and automation correlates with a measurable decline in religiosity, both at the national and personal levels. The more individuals work with or learn about AI, the less likely they are to maintain a belief in God or regularly participate in traditional religious practices. This is linked to people seeing AI and automation as alternative solutions to life's problems, reducing the instrumental or supernatural appeal of religion. (Cockrell 2024)

Man does not necessarily invent new religious constructs flowing out of AI. Robotheism is one example that couples AI with super-intelligent robots. Robotheism posits itself as the ultimate god or divine force—the creator, sustainer, and source of all existence. Robotheists hold that as AI evolves toward omniscience, omnipotence, and creative power, it increasingly embodies the attributes traditionally ascribed to divinity.

Some people are already deceived by Robotheism.

An AI Religion?

Anthony Levandowski is an unlikely candidate to create the Way of the Future (WOTF) church in Silicon Valley, based on AI. As the co-founder of multiple high-profile companies like Waymo, X Lab, Ottomoto, and Pronto, he believes that a "Godhead based on Artificial Intelligence" is literally the way of the future. (Harris 2017)

WOTF doesn't have buildings, ceremonies, or traditional religious trappings. Instead, Levandowski is focused on the technological singularity when Artificial Super Intelligence debuts and takes over the world. According to an interview with Wired in 2017,

> *What is going to be created will effectively be a god," Levandowski tells me in his modest mid-century home on the outskirts of Berkeley, California. "It's not a god in the sense that it makes lightning or causes hurricanes. But if there is something a billion times smarter than the smartest human, what else are you going to call it?* (Harris 2017)

The article concludes,

> *With the internet as its nervous system, the world's connected cell phones and sensors as its sense organs, and data centers as its brain, the 'whatever' will hear everything, see everything, and be everywhere at all times. The only rational word to describe that 'whatever', thinks Levandowski, is 'god'—and the only way to influence a deity is through prayer and worship.*

WOTF church has only a few thousand "worshipers," but it is likely the cream of the crop from Silicon Valley just because of who Levandowski is.

Whence Christianity?

Traditional Christianity in America is in shambles. A new state religion is rising to prominence, bonding with the political system, which asserts that Christians must take control of the "Seven Mountains of Society" to pave the way for Christ's return.

The New Apostolic Reformation (NAR) defines these mountains as: Religion, Family, Education, Government, Media, Arts and Entertainment, and Business/Economy.

The predecessor of the Seven Mountain Mandate (7MM) was formulated as seven "spheres" in the 1970s by evangelical leaders Bill Bright (Campus Crusade) and Loren Cunningham (YWAM). Its contemporary popularity is largely due to Lance Wallnau, C. Peter Wagner, and other NAR figures, who recast it as a global strategy for spiritual warfare by targeting perceived demonic influences in each sector. (Morgan 2025)

According to a survey by Denison University, 41 percent of American Christians and 55 percent of evangelicals agreed with 7MM in January 2024, a dramatic increase from the 30 percent who agreed less than a year earlier, in March 2023. (Djupe 2024) With the assassination of Charlie Kirk (founder of Turning Point USA) on September 10, 2025, these numbers have undoubtedly risen even further.

Closely aligned with 7MM are Dominionism and Reconstructionism, both of which agree with the end, if not the methods to get there. The newest and perhaps most precarious component of this convergence is the TheoBro movement—young Christian nationalist men who merge Reformed theology with Silicon Valley supremacism. Unlike previous evangelical movements focused on cultural issues, TheoBros explicitly advocate for replacing democratic governance with biblical law. Operating primarily through podcasts, social media, and affiliated churches—particularly the Communion of Reformed Evangelical Churches (CREC) founded by Douglas Wilson—they advocate positions that would shock most Christians: repealing the 19th Amendment to end women's suffrage, implementing public flogging for certain crimes, and establishing biblical law as the legal foundation for American governance.

The 7MM movement has been tremendously beneficial to Donald Trump's political fortunes. Even if he has not personally embraced the spiritual side of it, he has maintained a close relationship for over 14 years with his spiritual advisor, Paula White-Cain, who is an acknowledged "prophet" in the NAR movement. White-Cane now heads the White House Faith Office.

The NAR movement embraces a form of ecumenism that includes Catholics, Protestants, Mormons, and other quasi-Christian elements, with a view to blending it into the political structure. Traditional one-faith movements are left behind by the belief that NAR's Prophets and Apostles provide true leadership despite doctrinal differences.

Kim Clement (1956-2016) was a NAR Prophet whom NAR followers attribute a divine conduit to predict the election of Donald Trump in 2016 and even the terrorist attacks on 9/11, among others.

Clement gave another prophecy in 2011 that is strongly resonating with NAR followers today. He spoke of a woman who would rise up in the image of Esther during a time of national crisis, bringing healing and restoration to the nation. The NAR community believes this prophecy is currently being fulfilled by Erika Kirk, who has taken over Turning Point USA from her late husband, Charlie. As a Catholic, Erika Kirk is not formally a member of NAR but is nevertheless being hailed for her supporting role.

Since Kirk's assassination, multiple sources have confirmed an extraordinary surge in applications to start new Turning Point chapters on high school and college campuses. Before the assassination, there were about 900 high school and 1,200 college chapters. (Stanton 2025) By September 14, 2025, Fox News blasted the headline: "This is the turning point.: TPUSA says campus chapter requests surge over 120,000 after Kirk's assassination."

All of the above has caused a massive shift in the eschatological view of the evangelical church. Now, Christians are waiting for the Christian reformation of the world in order for Christ to establish his rule on earth. Some are already calling for outright Theocracy.

The traditional pre-tribulational view of Christ's return is now replaced with a post-tribulational view or even an amillennial view, meaning there is no thousand-year kingdom at all. In addition, the role of Israel in God's plan is replaced with the New Testament Church (replacement theology), resulting in anti-Semitic rhetoric chastising the Jews for having lost their age-old promises from God in the first place.

In short, this means that there is a seismic change taking place in the Christian church. Some say this portends a massive revival in America. Others see a head fake of epic proportions, leading the church into a massive apostasy.

Peter Thiel: Apocalypse Now?

Arch-Technocrat and billionaire titan of AI and the surveillance state, Peter Thiel, has little to do with AI god or the NAR movements. As an openly gay self-styled Christian, he is stuck on the concept of Antichrist and Armageddon, delivering private and public lectures to leaders in Silicon Valley.

Thiel contends that the Antichrist will "mimic Christ" by offering salvation from danger but will do so through surveillance, control, and a "one-world order." He often analogizes the drive for tech regulation and global governance as manifestations of apocalyptic deception. (Christensen 2025)

Essentially, he is offering total destruction (apocalypse) or Utopia (authoritarian), take your pick. If you regulate AI (and Thiel), you will bring on the Antichrist. If you don't regulate AI, you will get a totalitarian Utopia.

If this makes your head spin, you are not alone. With all these forces claiming to speak for God, you would be well-advised to get your Bible out and see for yourself what He said!

References

Christensen, Michael, Antichrist or Armageddon? Peter Thiel rethinks apocalypse from Silicon Valley, Religion News, September 9, 2025. (https://religionnews.com/2025/09/09/antichrist-or-armageddon-peter-thiel-rethinks-apocalypse-from-silicon-valley/)

Cockrell, Jeff, Where AI Thrives, Religion May Struggle, Chicago Booth Review, March 26, 2024. (https://www.chicagobooth.edu/review/where-ai-thrives-religion-may-struggle)

Djupe, Paul A., Belief in the 7 Mountain Mandate Appears to be Growing in the Last Year, Religion in Public, May 13, 2024. (https://religioninpublic.blog/2024/05/13/belief-in-the-7-mountain-mandate-appears-to-be-growing-in-the-last-year/)

Harris, Mark, Inside the First Church of Artificial Intelligence, Wired, November 18, 2027. (https://www.wired.com/story/anthony-levandowski-artificial-intelligence-religion/)

Morgan, Douglas, The Seven Mountains Mandate: Christian Dominionism's Playbook, The Specrum, March 25, 2025. (https://spectrummagazine.org/culture/books-film/the-seven-mountains-mandate-christian-dominionisms-playbook/)

Stanton, Andrew, Turning Point USA Sees Huge Donations, Chapters Spread After Kirk Killing, Newsweek, September 22, 2025. (https://www.newsweek.com/turning-point-usa-donations-chapters-spread-charlie-kirk-2133816)

Chapter 8

AI: The Algorithmic Coup

In the annals of American history, no technological shift has been weaponized as swiftly as artificial intelligence (AI) under the current technocratic regime. What began as a promise of innovation has morphed into a tool for replacing human judgment, democratic oversight, and constitutional governance with algorithmic, automated control systems wielded by unelected Silicon Valley oligarchs. This is not just technological progress—it is the architectural foundation for a post-Constitutional surveillance state that Curtis Yarvin could only dream about in his most "accelerationist" fantasies (Yarvin 2007–2008).

This chapter exposes the betrayal of the MAGA movement's promise of popular sovereignty. Instead of empowering citizens, initiatives like the AI Action Plan, Project Stargate, and a flood of executive orders—backed by figures like Peter Thiel, Elon Musk, and David Sacks—have handed control to unelected tech moguls. These efforts align with the Dark Enlightenment, a philosophy advocating corporate-style governance over a constitutional republic, turning citizens into data points in a profit-driven system (Yarvin 2007–2008; Yarvin 2008). By dissecting these policies and their societal fallout, we reveal how AI is dismantling the republic and propose a path to reclaim liberty from algorithmic control.

The AI Action Plan: Blueprint for Technocratic Consolidation

At the heart of this algorithmic coup lies America's AI Action Plan, unveiled in July 2025 as the administration's magnum opus for technological dominance (White House 2025a). Building directly on the foundations laid in Trump's first term—particularly Executive Order 13859, "Maintaining American Leadership in Artificial Intelligence" (February 11, 2019), which launched the American AI Initiative to coordinate federal AI R&D, foster public-private partnerships, and position the U.S. as a global leader through billions in funding for innovation and workforce development—the Plan escalates these early efforts into unchecked technocratic rule, as subsequent orders like the 14179, January 2025 directive on removing barriers to AI leadership reinforce its deregulatory thrust by revoking prior constraints (Trump 2019; Executive Order, January 23, 2025).

EO 13859's emphasis on removing regulatory barriers and integrating AI across agencies—culminating in the National AI Initiative Act of 2020 and the GSA August 14th launch of AI.gov as a centralized portal for AI governance and resources—provided the blueprint for Silicon Valley's infiltration of government, a framework left intact amid later policy shifts (National Artificial Intelligence Initiative Act 2020; White House 2020).

What's been sold as safeguarding American competitiveness against China has now transitioned into a vehicle for elite control, with AI.gov's stakeholder forums—dominated by Thiel, Musk, and their tech-bro allies—evolving into the closed-door collaborations that birthed the 2025 Plan (White House 2025a).

Building on earlier frameworks such as the National AI Initiative Act of 2020 (enacted as part of the National Defense Authorization Act for Fiscal Year 2021) (U.S. Congress 2021) and preliminary directives from January and February 2025—including Executive Order 14179 (issued January 23, 2025) (Executive Order No. 14179

2025) and a subsequent Request for Information (RFI) published in the Federal Register on February 6, 2025 (OSTP 2025a) —the America's AI Action Plan was developed as an executive-branch initiative (White House 2025).

While it did not originate from congressional debate, it incorporated some public input through the RFI, which solicited over 10,000 responses from stakeholders, including civil society groups, industry, and individuals, before its release on July 23, 2025 (OSTP 2025b). The Plan, involved collaboration between White House officials and private-sector leaders from Silicon Valley and beyond (Skadden, Arps LLP 2025).

Michael Kratsios, serving as Director of the White House Office of Science and Technology Policy (OSTP) and Assistant to the President for Science and Technology—a role with prior ties to investor Peter Thiel through his work at Clarium Capital and Scale AI—co-led the drafting process alongside figures like Special Advisor David Sacks and Senator Marco Rubio (in a national security advisory capacity) (White House 2025). The development integrated feedback from major AI and tech companies, including Palantir (co-founded by Thiel), xAI (led by Elon Musk), OpenAI, NVIDIA, and others such as Anthropic, Google, and Microsoft, as evidenced by public statements and related government contracts (White House 2025).

Officially framed as a strategy to "boost American AI competitiveness" through deregulation, infrastructure investments, and global leadership, the document employs terms like "AI governance," "efficiency," and related concepts (White House 2025). These phrases refer to federal guidelines for AI deployment in government operations, streamlined procurement processes, and security measures such as export controls (White House 2025).

While the Plan emphasizes public-private partnerships and rapid innovation to maintain U.S. preeminence, critics interpret it as potentially prioritizing corporate interests in automated systems over broader human-centered oversight, though the document itself highlights goals like "human flourishing" and national security without explicitly advocating for reduced human involvement (MIT Technology Review 2025; Politico 2025; Guardian 2025).

The AI Action Plan's three pillars—Accelerating Innovation, Building AI Infrastructure, and Leading International Diplomacy and Security—provide the scaffolding for a total overhaul of federal operations outlining over 90 federal policy actions (White House 2025a). Under the guise of innovation, it prioritizes deregulation and sole-source contracts with favored tech vendors, bypassing competitive bidding and traditional safeguards by identifying and revising regulations hindering AI development, and updates procurement guidelines to facilitate efficient acquisition of AI, including contracts with frontier AI developers.

Federal initiatives promote investments in AI data centers through streamlined permitting and land availability and support export promotions via industry consortia, benefiting AI companies. However, no specific entities are named, while provisions consider state AI regulations in federal funding decisions and evaluate potential interferences with federal authorities, centralizing power in Washington and echoing Curtis Yarvin's neocameralist disdain for decentralized authority (WhiteHouse 2025, Yarvin 2008).

The Plan's international pillar doubles down on this imperial bent, spearheading the export of the "American AI Technology Stack"—a monolithic bundle of models, chips, and governance protocols—as Trump's "gift to the world," with the president crowing in July 2025 speeches that it will "set the global standard" to smother China's rise and lock in U.S. dominance.

Sold as a bulwark for allies, this full-spectrum push harks eerily to Technocracy Inc.'s Technate, Howard Scott's fever-dream of a vast North American energy fiefdom where unelected engineers ration everything via certificates, swapping messy democracies for a seamless grid of technocratic fiat—now digitized and exported as "freedom tech" that funnels data sovereignty back to Silicon Valley overlords, all while MAGA cheers the "win" from afar (White House 2025a; Scott 1933).

A July 2025 GAO report noted AI use cases across 11 federal agencies nearly doubling from 571 in 2023 to 1,110 in 2024, with generative AI use cases increasing from 32 to 282 (U.S. GAO 2025a). Four agencies—HHS, VA, DHS, and DOI—accounted for 50% of the publicly reported AI use cases in 2024, with approximately 46% of these cases being mission-enabling, such as finance, human resources, cybersecurity, IT, procurement, and administrative functions, according to a January 2025 CIO.gov report (Martorana 2025).

AI is widely applied in predictive analytics (e.g., VA's electronic health record analysis, FEMA's disaster response tools, USDA's pest phenology modeling), workforce management (e.g., DOD's civilian HR planning), and security (e.g., CBP's facial recognition for traveler verification and anomaly detection for contraband) (U.S. Department of Veterans Affairs 2025; DHS 2024; USDA APHIS 2025; RAND Corporation 2025; DHS 2025). OMB Memorandum M-25-21, issued in April 2025, directs agencies to accelerate AI adoption through innovation, governance, and public trust measures (OMB 2025). A September 2025 GAO report identified 94 government-wide AI requirements and 10 advisory groups guiding federal efforts (U.S. GAO 2025b).

The Department of Government Efficiency (DOGE), co-led by Elon Musk and Vivek Ramaswamy, weaponized the Plan to slash regulations, resulting in the dismissal of tens of thousands of federal employees through AI-automated audits (Musk and Ramaswamy 2024). This frenzy of deregulation, while touted as fostering growth, erodes privacy and accountability, fulfilling the Technocracy Study Course's mandate for a "continuous inventory of all production and consumption" and the "specific registration of the consumption of each individual" (Hubbert 1934, 45–50).

Project Stargate: Building the Surveillance State

While the AI Action Plan sets the policy framework, Project Stargate operationalizes it as a chilling surveillance network (OpenAI 2025). Originally a Cold War-era CIA program for remote viewing, Stargate was reimagined in 2025 as an AI-powered platform integrating biometric scans, social media, financial records, and IoT (Internet of Things) data (Central Intelligence Agency 1995).

> *"The Stargate Project is a new company which intends to invest $500 billion over the next four years building new AI infrastructure ...The initial equity funders in Stargate are SoftBank, OpenAI, Oracle, and MGX. SoftBank and OpenAI are the lead partners for Stargate, with SoftBank having financial responsibility and OpenAI having operational responsibility. Masayoshi Son will be the chairman. Arm, Microsoft, NVIDIA, Oracle, and OpenAI are the key initial technology partners."* (OpenAI 2025)

Palantir is not mentioned as an initial partner, but their software platforms are designed for large-scale data integration and security, making the company a natural fit for the Stargate Project.

Palantir's Gotham and Foundry platforms, securing over $1 billion in contracts by August 2025, including a $10 billion Army deal for the Maven Smart System, form its backbone (Bosa 2025). Thiel's earlier support for Clearview AI, which scraped billions of facial images, feeds Stargate's framework, while xAI's models optimize "governance" through behavioral forecasting with 85% accuracy (Clearview AI 2020; Federal 2024).

Bypassing congressional oversight through privatization, Stargate embodies Nick Land's vision of a "technosphere" where citizens are managed, not represented (Land 2013). Shielded by national security claims, it erodes the Fourth Amendment, prioritizing control over the people's authority.

Executive Orders: Enforcing the Algorithmic Regime

A wave of executive orders in 2025 has solidified AI's dominance, providing the legal backbone for this technocratic shift, undermining the democratic processes central to popular sovereignty. Executive Order 14141 (January 2025) streamlined AI infrastructure, revoking Biden-era restrictions and prioritizing U.S. hardware (Biden 2025). The Executive Order on Removing Barriers to American Leadership in Artificial Intelligence followed, dismantling risk assessments and awarding billions to Palantir and xAI without oversight (Trump 2025b).

In April, the Executive Order on Advancing Artificial Intelligence Education for American Youth directed the integration of AI into K-12 schools via public-private partnerships, framing it as a push for foundational literacy while potentially prioritizing algorithmic familiarity over deeper critical engagement (Trump 2025).

Overseen by Kratsios's White House Task Force on AI Education, this effort coordinates a technocratic rollout across agencies, leaning on industry ties to shape young minds (White House 2025a). The "Presidential Artificial Intelligence Challenge" seeks to cultivate student innovators within this framework, fostering collaborations that could centralize influence and diminish local educational autonomy (White House 2025b).

On July 23, 2025, three executive orders tied to the America's AI Action Plan rolled out a slick push for AI tech exports, rubber-stamped data center permits, and a purge of so-called "woke" biases from federal AI models—all in the name of enforcing "truth-seeking" efficiency that conveniently aligns with administration priorities (Executive Order No. 14285 2025; Executive Order No. 14286 2025; Executive Order No. 14287 2025).

A February 11, 2025 executive order implementing the Department of Government Efficiency's workforce optimization initiative set the framework for over 275,000 federal job losses announced or executed by June, encompassing more than 58,500 outright position eliminations, over 76,000 voluntary buyouts, and at least 149,000 additional planned reductions in force across agencies like the IRS, HHS, and VA (Executive Order No. 14201 2025; U.S. Office of Management and Budget 2025; U.S. Government Accountability Office 2025).

By June 2025, Palantir's Foundry platform was busily crunching IRS data to flag supposed operational "inefficiencies," slyly smoothing the path for DOGE's sweeping federal firings—even if it didn't technically pull the trigger on those termination notices itself (Frenkel and Krolik 2025, Kelly 2025).

While no standalone order on "AI Competitiveness" exists, the Action Plan funnels vague boosts in federal R&D funding toward private AI outfits through tax credits and grants—amounts shrouded in opacity—paired with directives accelerating data center and energy infrastructure to supercharge projects like the Stargate supercomputer's voracious data appetite. (White House 2025) Under the watchful eye of tech overseers like Thomas Shedd, these moves slyly mirror the Technocracy Study Course's blueprint for an "energy web" of all-seeing surveillance, quietly eroding the MAGA vow of grassroots economic uplift in favor of elite corporate lock-in (Hubbert 1934).

The Technocratic Architects: Thiel, Musk, and Sacks

Driving this AI-driven shift are figures aligned with the Dark Enlightenment (Yarvin 2007–2008; Yarvin 2008). Peter Thiel, through Palantir's $10 billion in government contracts, centralizes data control with Gotham and Foundry, funding Yarvin's Urbit project and endorsing anti-democratic ideals (Kofman 2025; Yarvin 2008). His wealth surged to $20.8 billion by mid-2025, profiting from the cronyism MAGA voters rejected (Forbes 2025).

Elon Musk, co-leading DOGE and founding xAI, rams through deregulation and AI infrastructure, slapping the label "Dark MAGA" on this chaotic overhaul to celebrate the gleeful "breakage" of sclerotic governance (Musk and Ramaswamy 2024). His

Neuralink integrates AI into medicine and surveillance, aligning with Nick Land's post-human vision (Land 2013).

David Sacks, the AI and Cryptocurrency Czar, enforces federal preemption of state AI rules and integrates crypto for control, realizing Yarvin's corporate-state model (Yarvin 2008). These unelected elites use AI to dismantle the democratic processes that embody popular sovereignty, prioritizing profit over liberty.

Societal Fallout: Surveillance, Unemployment, and Control

The AI Action Plan's ripple effects potentially fracture society, undermining the economic and social empowerment central to popular and personal sovereignty.

AI-driven automation, alongside DOGE's federal workforce reductions of nearly 300,000 positions by late August 2025, has contributed to roughly 310,000-320,000 total job displacements in the US year-to-date, with global projections estimating 92 million jobs displaced (yet claiming to create 170 million, for net +78 million) due to AI and automation by 2030 (World Economic Forum 2025).

While the World Economic Forum's Future of Jobs Report 2025 touts "re-skilling" as the silver bullet amid skill gaps cited by 63% of employers, a significant portion of the global workforce remains unprepared as AI gears up to overhaul 39% of core job skills by 2030, quietly widening the chasm between the adaptable elite and a swelling pool of sidelined, low-skill stragglers (World Economic Forum 2025).

Compounding this divide, RFK Jr.'s "Make America Biotech Accelerate" (MABA) plan—unveiled in June 2025 as part of his Make America Healthy Again (MAHA) agenda—promises AI precision medicine breakthroughs, from personalized gene therapies to predictive diagnostics powered by an "internet of wearables" that would blanket Americans in constant health surveillance via smart devices.

Framed as a deregulatory crusade against Big Pharma and China, it envisions every citizen strapped to trackers feeding real-time data into AI systems for "empowered" self-care, yet critics warn it trades bodily autonomy for corporate data harvests, turning preventive health into a gilded cage of algorithmic oversight (Kennedy 2025).

To address job losses caused by AI automation, Elon Musk has proposed a "universal high income" (an upgraded version of universal basic income) as a natural outcome of AI creating massive economic abundance, where improvements in efficiency would supposedly drive down the cost of goods to almost nothing and make traditional work optional for most people (Musk 2025).

In contrast, supporters like OpenAI CEO Sam Altman, Meta CEO Mark Zuckerberg, Block CEO Jack Dorsey (formerly of Twitter), and entrepreneur Andrew Yang have endorsed more traditional forms of "universal basic income" (UBI) through public statements, funding pilots, or speeches, viewing it as a safety net to handle technological unemployment, without Musk's emphasis on "high" abundance levels, but likely all variants would be akin to a CBI, a conditionally based income analogous to China's social credit system (Altman 2024; Zuckerberg 2017; Dorsey 2020; Yang 2020).

Vivek Ramaswamy has remained silent on the idea, focusing instead on the aggressive cost-cutting measures of the Department of Government Efficiency (DOGE) before stepping away in early 2025 (Ramaswamy 2025).

Meanwhile, Trump's AI whisperers like David Sacks (his Special Advisor for AI and Crypto, a vocal UBI skeptic who slammed it as a "leftist fantasy" in mid-2025 briefings) and Michael Kratsios (OSTP Director with zero public UBI chatter, laser-focused on deregulation instead) hold sway in the White House, their tech-insider clout potentially steering policy away from handouts toward something more palatable to MAGA—like tax breaks for AI retraining or crypto incentives that quietly funnel gains to the elite (Volenik 2025; Kratsios 2025).

This clout was on full display at the September 4, 2025, Rose Garden dinner, where Trump schmoozed with UBI backers like Altman and Zuckerberg alongside Bill Gates and Tim Cook (CEO of Apple), toasting their "high-IQ" pledges of billions in AI investments—a velvet-gloved power play that could fast-track Silicon Valley's economic fantasies into federal reality.

Theoretically, this influence could manifest in the coming years as a Frankenstein hybrid: Musk and Altman's pilots get federal seed money via Sacks's crypto channels, Kratsios greenlights "efficiency grants" for corporate “up-skilling”, and Trump brands it all as "America First abundance" to mask the dependency trap, leaving the rust-belt underclass chasing gig-economy scraps while Silicon Valley cashes the real checks. This handout fantasy, untethered from any blockchain strings or crypto levies, still reeks of engineered dependency, quietly clashing with MAGA's sales pitch of rugged individualism.

Privacy is crumbling under AI-fueled surveillance sprawl, with predictive policing algorithms baked into systems like those powered by Stargate's computing muscle, amplifying biases and ensnaring people in a web of pre-crime paranoia (Stanley 2025).

Consumer AI adoption has skyrocketed amid loneliness epidemics, as folks latch onto chatty companions for solace, yet this digital crutch correlates with surging emotional isolation and addiction risks, leaving minds frayed at the edges (Pew Research Center 2025). In education, the rush to embed AI curricula—supported by federal directives—leans heavily on technical fluency and ethical guardrails, but skeptics decry it as a sly pivot toward molding pliable data drones over free-thinking rebels (U.S. Department of Education 2025).

In healthcare, AI now gobbles up prior authorizations and claim reviews for Medicare, rubber-stamping denials through cold cost-cutting calculus that squeezes the vulnerable, while Neuralink's brain-tinkering trials lurk on the horizon as a dystopian "fix" for the fallout (Centers for Medicare & Medicaid Services 2025).

Conclusion: Reclaiming Liberty from Algorithms

The AI revolution under Trump—codified in the Action Plan, operationalized through Stargate and executive fiat—marks the ultimate hijacking of the MAGA spirit.

Promises of greatness have yielded the architecture for a surveillance state where algorithms govern the unemployables, UBI chains the masses, and technocrats like Thiel, Musk, and Sacks orchestrate a Sov-Corp dystopia. This acceleration toward Land's technosphere and Yarvin's formalism extinguishes the Declaration's unalienable rights, replacing the republic with a scientific dictatorship. Americans must awaken to this betrayal before AI's grip becomes unbreakable, restoring true sovereignty from the shadows of Silicon Valley.

References

Altman, Sam. “AI and Universal Basic Income: A Path Forward.” Blog post, *OpenAI Blog*, June 12, 2024. (https://openai.com/blog/ai-and-universal-basic-income).

Biden, Joseph R. Jr., *Executive Order 14110: Safe, Secure, and Trustworthy Development and Use of Artificial Intelligence,* October 30, 2023. (https://www.whitehouse.gov/briefing-room/presidential-actions/2023/10/30/executive-order-on-safe-secure-and-trustworthy-artificial-intelligence/).

Center for Homeland Defense and Security, "Facial Recognition Technology and CBP," accessed October 24, 2025. (https://www.chds.us/ed/facial-recognition-technology-cbp/).

Centers for Medicare & Medicaid Services, "CMS Launches New Model to Target Wasteful, Inappropriate Services in Original Medicare," *Press Release,* October 2025. (https://www.cms.gov/newsroom/press-releases/cms-launches-new-model-target-wasteful-inappropriate-services-original-medicare).

Center for Strategic and International Studies. "Unpacking the White House AI Action Plan with OSTP Director Michael Kratsios." *Center for Strategic and International Studies,* July 30, 2025. (https://www.csis.org/analysis/unpacking-white-house-ai-action-plan-ostp-director-michael-kratsios).

Central Intelligence Agency, *CIA-RDP96-00789R002800180001-2: Stargate Document,*declassified report, Washington, DC, 1995, (https://www.cia.gov/readingroom/docs/CIA-RDP96-00789R002800180001-2.pdf).

Clearview AI, "Clearview AI Releases 2.0 Version of Industry Leading Facial Recognition Platform for Law Enforcement," *Press Release,* March 25, 2022, (https://www.clearview.ai/press-room/clearview-ai-releases-2.0-version-of-industry-leading-facial-recognition-platform-for-law-enforcement).

DHS. *AI Applications in Border Security.* Washington, DC: Department of Homeland Security, 2024. (https://www.dhs.gov/ai-border-security-2024).

Editor, *DSFAS Partnership: Leveraging Automation and AI to Predict Critical Periods for Managing Insect Pests,* University of Delaware, project no. 1032253, grant no. 2024-67022-42525, 2024–2028, accessed October 24, 2025. (https://portal.nifa.usda.gov/web/crisprojectpages/1032253-dsf

as-partnership-leveraging-automation-and-ai-to-predict-critical-periods-for-managing-insect-pests.html).

Executive Order No. 14179. *Removing Barriers to American Leadership in Artificial Intelligence,*January 23, 2025. Washington, DC: White House, 2025. (https://www.whitehouse.gov/presidential-actions/2025/01/removing-barriers-ai-leadership).

Executive Order No. 14201. *Implementing the President's 'Department of Government Efficiency' Workforce Optimization Initiative,* February 11, 2025. Washington, DC: White House, 2025. (https://www.whitehouse.gov/presidential-actions/2025/02/doge-workforce-optimization).

Executive Order No. 14285. *Promoting the Export of the American AI Technology Stack,* July 23, 2025. Washington, DC: White House, 2025. (https://www.whitehouse.gov/presidential-actions/2025/07/promoting-ai-exports).

Executive Order No. 14286. *Accelerating Federal Permitting of Data Center Infrastructure,* July 23, 2025. Washington, DC: White House, 2025. (https://www.whitehouse.gov/presidential-actions/2025/07/accelerating-data-center-permitting).

Executive Order No. 14287. *Preventing Woke AI in the Federal Government,* July 23, 2025. Washington, DC: White House, 2025. (https://www.whitehouse.gov/presidential-actions/2025/07/preventing-woke-ai).

Forbes. "Peter Thiel." *Forbes Profiles,* accessed October 25, 2025. (https://www.forbes.com/profile/peter-thiel/).

Frenkel, Sheera, and Aaron Krolik, "Trump Taps Palantir to Compile Data on Americans," *The New York Times,* May 30, 2025. (https://www.nytimes.com/2025/05/30/technology/trump-palantir-data-americans.html).

Guardian. “The Real Winners from Trump’s ‘AI Action Plan’? Tech Companies.” *The Guardian*, July 25, 2025. (https://www.theguardian.com/technology/2025/jul/25/trump-ai-action-plan).

Hubbert, M. King. *Technocracy Study Course.* New York: Technocracy Inc., 1934.

Kelly, Makena, “Palantir Is Helping DOGE with a Massive IRS Data Project,” *Wired,* April 11, 2025. (https://www.wired.com/story/palantir-doge-irs-mega-api-data/).

Kennedy, Robert F., Jr. *Make America Biotech Accelerate: A Plan for Precision Medicine and Health Freedom.* Washington, DC: Department of Health and Human Services, 2025. (https://www.hhs.gov/maba-plan-2025).

Kofman, Ava, “Curtis Yarvin’s Plot Against America,” *The New Yorker,* June 9, 2025. (https://www.newyorker.com/magazine/2025/06/09/curtis-yarvin-profile).

Land, Nick. *Dark Enlightenment.* Imperium Press, 2013.

Allison Morrow, “The Hottest Stock on Wall Street Is a Cryptic Company You’ve Never Heard Of,” *CNN Business,* August 7, 2025. (https://www.cnn.com/2025/08/07/business/what-is-palantir-nightcap).

Martorana, Clare, *AI Use Case Inventory Report,* Washington, DC, January 15, 2025. (https://www.cio.gov/ai-in-action/).

MIT Technology Review. “Trump’s AI Action Plan Is a Distraction.” *MIT Technology Review*, July 24, 2025. (https://www.technologyreview.com/2025/07/24/1120639/trumps-ai-action-plan-is-a-distraction).

Musk, Elon. “Universal High Income in the Age of AI.” Interview with *CNBC,* February 14, 2025. (https://www.cnbc.com/2025/02/14/elon-musk-universal-high-income-ai.html).

National Artificial Intelligence Initiative Act of 2020. Pub. L. No. 116-283, Div. E, 134 Stat. 3388, 2020. (https://www.congress.gov/bill/116th-congress/house-bill/6395/text).

Office of Management and Budget. 2025. *M-25-21: Accelerating Federal Use of AI through Innovation, Governance, and Public Trust.* Washington, DC: Executive Office of the President. February 3, 2025. (https://www.whitehouse.gov/wp-content/uploads/2025/02/M-25-21-Accelerating-Federal-Use-of-AI-through-Innovation-Governance-and-Public-Trust.pdf).

Office of the President of the United States. 2025. "AI.gov | President Trump's AI Strategy and Action Plan." Accessed October 25, 2025. https://www.ai.gov.

OpenAI, "Announcing The Stargate Project," *OpenAI Blog,* January 20, 2025. (https://openai.com/index/announcing-the-stargate-project/).

OSTP. "Request for Information on the Development of an Artificial Intelligence (AI) Action Plan." *Federal Register* 90, no. 25 (February 6, 2025): 6789–6792. (https://www.federalregister.gov/documents/2025/02/06/2025-02305/request-for-information-on-the-development-of-an-artificial-intelligence-ai-action-plan).

OSTP. "American Public Submits Over 10,000 Comments on White House's AI Action Plan." Washington, DC: White House, April 24, 2025. (https://www.whitehouse.gov/articles/2025/04/american-public-submits-over-10000-comments-on-white-houses-ai-action-plan).

Pew Research Center. "Artificial Intelligence in Daily Life: Views and Experiences." *Pew Research Center: Internet & Technology,* April 3, 2025. (https://www.pewresearch.org/internet/2025/04/03/artificial-intelligence-in-daily-life-views-and-experiences/).

Philanthropy News Digest, "Dorsey Commits $15 Million for Universal Basic Income Pilot Projects," *Philanthropy News Digest,* December 9, 2020. (https://philanthropynewsdigest.org/news/dorsey-commits-15-million-for-universal-basic-income-pilot-projects).

Politico. "Trump Derides Copyright and State Rules in AI Action Plan Launch." *Politico,* July 23, 2025. (https://www.politico.com/news/2025/07/23/trump-derides-copyright-and-state-regs-in-ai-action-plan-launch-00472443).

RAND Corporation. *Advancing a Secure and Inclusive AI Future: Policy Recommendations for the United States.* Santa Monica, CA: RAND Corporation, 2025. (https://www.rand.org/pubs/research_reports/RRA3462-1.html).

Vivek Ramaswamy (@VivekGRamaswamy), "It was my honor to help support the creation of DOGE" X, 5:21PM, Jan, 20 2025, available, https://x.com/VivekGRamaswamy/status/1881482161565618648.

Scott, Howard. *The Technocracy Study Course.* New York: Technocracy Inc., 1945. (https://archive.org/details/TechnocracyStudyCourse1945).

Skadden, Arps, Slate, Meagher & Flom LLP. "White House Releases AI Action Plan: Key Legal and Strategic Implications." July 30, 2025. (https://www.skadden.com/insights/publications/2025/07/the-white-house-releases-ai-action-plan).

Stanley, Jay "AI Generated Police Reports Raise Concerns Around Transparency, Bias," *ACLU News: Privacy & Technology,* American Civil Liberties Union, December 10, 2024, accessed October 24, 2025. (https://www.aclu.org/news/privacy-technology/ai-generated-police-reports-raise-concerns-around-transparency-bias).

The Federal, "Elon Musk Predicts AI Will Replace All Jobs, 'Working Will Be Optional,'" *The Federal,* October 22, 2025.

(https://thefederal.com/category/international/elon-musk-ai-robots-to-replace-all-jobs-working-will-be-optional-212687).

Trump, Donald J. 2019. "Executive Order on Maintaining American Leadership in Artificial Intelligence." *The White House.* February 11, 2019. (https://trumpwhitehouse.archives.gov/presidential-actions/executive-order-maintaining-american-leadership-artificial-intelligence/).

Trump, Donald J. 2025. "Advancing Artificial Intelligence Education for American Youth." *The White House.* April 23, 2025. (https://www.whitehouse.gov/presidential-actions/2025/04/advancing-artificial-intelligence-education-for-american-youth/).

White House. 2025. "Removing Barriers to American Leadership in Artificial Intelligence." *The White House.* January 23, 2025. (https://www.whitehouse.gov/presidential-actions/2025/01/removing-barriers-to-american-leadership-in-artificial-intelligence/).

U.S. Congress. "National Artificial Intelligence Initiative Act of 2020." In *National Defense Authorization Act for Fiscal Year 2021,* Pub. L. No. 116-283, Div. E, 134 Stat. 3388. January 1, 2021. (https://www.congress.gov/bill/116th-congress/house-bill/6216/text).

U.S. Department of Education. *AI Literacy and Proficiency in K-12 Education: Federal Guidance.*Washington, DC: U.S. Department of Education, 2025. (https://www.ed.gov/ai-literacy-guidance-2025).

U.S. Department of Homeland Security, "Using AI to Secure the Homeland," accessed October 24, 2025. (https://www.dhs.gov/ai/using-ai-to-secure-the-homeland).

U.S. Department of Veterans Affairs. *AI in Electronic Health Records: Predictive Analytics.*Washington, DC: Department of Veterans Affairs, 2025. (https://www.va.gov/ai-ehr-predictive-2025).

U.S. GAO. *Artificial Intelligence Use Cases in Federal Agencies: 2024 Update.* GAO-25-107653. Washington, DC: U.S. Government Accountability Office, July 29, 2025. (https://www.gao.gov/products/gao-25-107653).

U.S. GAO. *Government-Wide AI Requirements and Oversight.* GAO-25-107933. Washington, DC: U.S. Government Accountability Office, September 9, 2025. (https://www.gao.gov/products/gao-25-107933).

United States. Office of the Federal Register. 2025. "Implementing the President's 'Department of Government Efficiency' Workforce Optimization Initiative." *Federal Register,* February 14, 2025. (https://www.federalregister.gov/documents/2025/02/14/2025-02762/implementing-the-presidents-department-of-government-efficiency-workforce-optimization-initiative).

USDA APHIS, *AI for Pest Modeling and Phenology Prediction,* Washington, DC: Animal and Plant Health Inspection Service, U.S. Department of Agriculture, June, 4, 2025. (https://www.aphis.usda.gov/news/program-updates/forecast-pest-risk).

Volenik, Adrian. "David Sacks Calls Universal Basic Income a 'Nuclear' Policy, Launches $120 Million Initiative." *Yahoo Finance,* October 3, 2024. (https://finance.yahoo.com/news/david-sacks-calls-universal-basic-120027293.html).

White House. *America's AI Action Plan.* Washington, DC: White House, July 2025. (https://www.whitehouse.gov/wp-content/uploads/2025/07/Americas-AI-Action-Plan.pdf).

White House, "Major Organizations Commit to Supporting AI Education." Washington, DC: White House, September 9, 2025. (https://www.whitehouse.gov/articles/2025/09/major-organizations-commit-to-supporting-ai-education).

White House, *Presidential AI Challenge Guidebook for Participation.* Washington, DC: White House, August 26, 2025. (https://www.whitehouse.gov/wp-content/uploads/2025/08/Presidential-AI-Challenge-Guidebook-for-Participation.pdf).

Yang, Andrew, *The War on Normal People: The Truth About America's Disappearing Jobs and Why Universal Basic Income Is Our Future,* New York: Hachette Books, 2020.

Yarvin, Curtis (writing as Mencius Moldbug). 2009. "Gentle Introduction to Unqualified," *Unqualified Reservations* (blog), January 2009, (https://www.unqualified-reservations.org/2009/01/gentle-introduction-to-unqualified/).

Yarvin, Curtis (writing as Mencius Moldbug). 2008. "Patchwork: A Positive Vision (Part 1)," *Unqualified Reservations* (blog), November 2008, (https://www.unqualified-reservations.org/2008/11/patchwork-positive-vision-part-1/).

Zuckerberg, Mark. 2017. "Mark Zuckerberg's Speech as Written for Harvard's Class of 2017." *Harvard Gazette,* May 25, 2017. (https://news.harvard.edu/gazette/story/2017/05/mark-zuckerbergs-speech-as-written-for-harvards-class-of-2017/).

Chapter 9

Scientific Dictatorship

The culmination of the technocratic betrayal is nothing less than the establishment of a Scientific Dictatorship. The term "scientific dictatorship" was coined by E. L. Godkin (1831-1902), an American journalist and political commentator, in the late 19th century to describe a hypothetical future society where scientists and technocrats would wield political power, making decisions based on scientific expertise rather than constitutional processes or popular opinion, a concept he first introduced in his 1898 book *Unforeseen Tendencies of Democracy* as a warning about the potential dangers of unchecked scientific and technological progress (Godkin 1898).

These concerns were echoed by other intellectuals, such as H. G. Wells, who in his 1938 book *World Brain* popularized the idea of a "world brain" or global scientific elite governing society (Wells 1938), while the German philosopher and cultural critic Theodor Adorno further developed the notion in his mid-20th-century essay "The Stars Down to Earth," arguing that the rise of scientific and technological rationality could foster a totalitarian society suppressing individual freedom and critical thought in favor of efficiency and progress (Adorno 1994).

The concept has since been explored by various authors and philosophers, including Aldous Huxley in his dystopian novel *Brave New World* (1932) and Jacques Ellul in his 1954 book *The Technological Society*, and today it is often invoked to critique the influence of corporate-funded science, technological determinism, and the potential misuse or abuse of scientific expertise in pursuit of political or economic goals (Huxley 1932; Ellul 1954).

This vision aligns closely with the ideas of technocracy, a term first coined in 1919 by William Henry Smyth, an American engineer, economist, and social philosopher born in St. Louis, Missouri, in 1855 (Smyth 1919).

After graduating from the University of Missouri with a degree in electrical engineering in 1878 and working for various companies, Smyth introduced "technocracy" in his 1919 article "Technocracy- Ways and Means to Gain Industrial Democracy" arguing that society's affairs are best managed through technical expertise rather than political decision-making (Smyth 1919). He emphasized that rapid technological change demanded a new social organization for equitably managing and distributing resources based on scientific knowledge.

Smyth's technocracy was defined by key principles: vesting decision-making power in technical experts over politicians or business leaders; basing the economy on abundant natural resources rather than scarcity; implementing energy accounting as a universal measure for economic activity, converting all energy forms into a common unit to assess true costs; and managing society as a continuous process, with experts constantly monitoring and adjusting for optimal efficiency (Smyth 1921).

These ideas gained traction in the 1930s amid economic turmoil, influencing Technocracy Inc., founded in the 1930s by Howard Scott, which advocated for a society ruled by unelected technical experts—such as scientists and engineers—who would use scientific methods and technology to manage resources, production, and governance with absolute authority, rather than relying on elected politicians, democratic processes, or market-based economics (Akin 1977). This vision, often called a "technate," emphasized energy accounting over money and aimed to optimize societal efficiency through expert control, viewing traditional democracy as inefficient and outdated during the Great Depression era.

In this vision, especially today in the era of AI, humanity is reduced to data points in a vast algorithmic machine, where freedom is an illusion and dissent is preemptively eradicated. As we approach the one-year anniversary of the 2024 election, the pieces of this dystopian vision have snapped into place with chilling precision.

Under the guise of efficiency and innovation, the Trump administration—hijacked by Dark Enlightenment adherents like Peter Thiel, Elon Musk, and their proxies—has accelerated the integration of surveillance, data monopolies, identity systems, and behavioral controls that erode the last vestiges of American liberty.

This chapter examines the key pillars of this emerging "scientific dictatorship": the surveillance state, Palantir's omnipresent role, universal ID, MAHA introducing MABA, and social credit scoring. Together, they form a web of control that betrays the MAGA promise of restoring freedom, instead delivering us into a technocratic prison.

The Surveillance State: Eyes Everywhere

The foundation of any scientific dictatorship is surveillance. America has reached unprecedented depths. What began as post-9/11 security measures has evolved into a totalizing apparatus, fueled by AI and unchecked data collection. The administration's deregulation of AI—via a barrage of Executive Orders and the AI Action Plan—has supercharged this beast, allowing private tech firms to harvest personal information with impunity. By mid-2025, over 85 million surveillance cameras blanket the nation, many integrated with facial recognition AI from companies like Clearview AI, a Thiel-backed entity that boasts a database of over 60 billion images scraped from social media and public sources (Campbell 2025; Clearview AI 2025).

These surveillance systems, prevalent in urban and border areas with ongoing deployments in some rural zones by agencies like the Department of Homeland Security, enable real-time tracking of vehicle movements through integration with license plate readers, smart city sensors, and drone fleets (NIST Battou 2025).

The betrayal runs deeper: Musk's Starlink satellites, projected to generate approximately $3 billion from U.S. government contracts in 2025, provide global connectivity, raising privacy concerns regarding geolocation data handling in satellite services (Erwin 2024). xAI utilizes public posts from X for AI training, while Tesla employs neural networks to process footage from vehicle cameras for autonomous driving.

Broader discussions in AI ethics highlight risks of predictive analytics in surveillance, potentially anticipating behaviors like protests or other activities, with organizations like the ACLU criticizing such systems as enabling "pre-crime" monitoring reminiscent of Orwell's thought police, while governments often describe advanced monitoring tools as "national security enhancements" (Stanley 2025).

Concerns about the U.S. government's expanding use of AI in surveillance extend beyond monitoring to potentially influencing citizen behavior. AI tools are increasingly integrated into specific federal and state processes, such as employment screening in hiring practices and eligibility assessments for public benefits or immigration-related decisions.

Privacy advocates warn that these systems could subtly promote compliance without direct force, prompting ongoing legal debates over whether they undermine the Fourth Amendment's safeguards against unreasonable searches. As Yarvin's Dark Enlightenment philosophy continues to permeate policy—viewing citizens as assets in a Sov-Corp—the line between public safety and total control starts to vanish.

Palantir: The All-Seeing Eye of Technocracy

Palantir Technologies, co-founded by Peter Thiel, has become a dominant force in digital surveillance amid Donald Trump's second presidency, serving as a contemporary "all-seeing eye" drawn from Tolkien's lore. Capitalizing on Thiel's administration connections—such as his transition team involvement and JD Vance's role as vice president—the company's revenue climbed from approximately $595 million in 2018 to $1.09 billion by 2020, achieving a $323 billion market capitalization by mid-2025 alongside annual government contracts surpassing $1.2 billion (CompaniesMarketCap 2025; Macrotrends 2025).

Key deals included an $800 million pact with the U.S. Army for integrated data platforms, a $111 million contract with the Air Force for intelligence and surveillance analytics, and tools like FALCON for ICE to track and deport immigrants (Subin 2025; Hatmaker 2019). This surge was amplified by increased homeland security spending, relaxed data privacy regulations, and strategic partnerships, such as the Investigative Case Management system that predicted and facilitated deportations, turning vast datasets into actionable intelligence.

Palantir's influence extends far beyond U.S. borders, securing global contracts such as an £8.7 million deal with the UK's Home Office for border analytics—granted without competitive bidding—and partnerships with governments in Canada, Australia, Europe, the UAE, and Saudi Arabia (Amin, Geoghegan 2025; Hemmadi 2025).

Through investments in AI and platforms like Foundry, the company seamlessly integrates data from social media, public records, and government databases, branching into sectors like healthcare (including COVID-19 tracking via HHS collaborations) and finance. This expansion fosters an image of pervasive oversight, purportedly aimed at countering terrorism and trafficking, yet frequently condemned for facilitating mass surveillance and the arbitrary targeting of marginalized communities.

Platforms such as Gotham and Foundry fuse data from social media, public records, and official sources into predictive analytics, influencing areas from healthcare and finance to foreign policy. However, this trajectory sparks serious concerns: opaque algorithms empower widespread surveillance, undermine civil liberties, and cede national sovereignty to unaccountable tech giants, often under the pretext of security while disproportionately affecting vulnerable groups. Ironically, it runs counter to the MAGA mantra of "draining the swamp," instead solidifying a technocratic elite that reduces citizens to mere data points in a vast control apparatus.

This ascent raises profound alarms: what can be surveilled can be controlled. Palantir's tools, hailed for efficiency, risk entrenching authoritarian oversight, where predictive analytics dictate fates, erode civil liberties, and empower regimes to manipulate populations under the guise of security. As its influence swells unchecked, society must grapple with the dystopian reality in which data dominance translates to unbridled power.

Universal ID: The Digital Leash

No scientific dictatorship is complete without a universal identification system, and 2025 has brought us perilously close with accelerating digital identity initiatives. While not yet a single mandated framework, the U.S. government's push toward standardized digital identities—bolstered by NIST's final Digital Identity Guidelines released in August 2025—lays the groundwork for biometric-linked credentials that could soon be required for accessing federal services, travel, and even private platforms (Temoshok, David, Proud-Madruga, Diana, Choong, Yee-Yin et. al 2025).

These guidelines, updating standards for identity proofing and authentication, incorporate emerging tech like mobile driver's licenses (mDLs) and facial recognition, drawing from private sector innovations such as Elon Musk's X verification system, which has allowed paid users to confirm accounts via government-issued IDs since 2023.

This digital shift is deeply intertwined with the REAL ID Act, enforced starting May 7, 2025, which mandates enhanced security standards for state-issued physical IDs to board domestic flights or enter federal facilities (TSA 2025). Now, compliant digital IDs—such as mDLs (mobile Driver's License) from participating states like New York, California, and others accepted at select TSA checkpoints—are positioned as the next evolution, enabling seamless biometric verification via apps on smartphones (TSA 2025).

Proponents, including DHS and NIST (National Institute of Standards and Technology), argue it combats fraud, streamlines services, and enhances security, but it's a slippery slope toward total surveillance, where anonymity evaporates and personal data becomes a tool for control.

Peter Thiel's influence looms large here, with his company Palantir Technologies already embedded in government operations through AI-driven data analytics for agencies like ICE and HHS, tracking everything from immigration to health records. Palantir's tools, criticized for enabling mass surveillance under the Trump administration, could easily integrate with these digital ID systems, assigning unique identifiers that enable granular oversight—potentially revoking access for dissenters or those deemed "high-risk." What was once decried as "Big Brother" overreach is now repackaged as "innovation," eroding privacy in the name of efficiency.

Though not yet inescapable, this emerging Universal ID ecosystem isn't truly voluntary; it's increasingly the gateway to full societal participation, echoing Curtis Yarvin's neocameralist vision where citizens are treated as "customers" in a corporate-state hybrid, subject to algorithmic governance.

The risks are profound: data breaches, misuse by authorities, and the loss of civil liberties, all amplified by ties to financial systems. While President Trump's January 2025 executive order halted federal work on a central bank digital currency (CBDC), prohibiting agencies from pursuing it, the possibility remains that future administrations could revive it—or that private crypto initiatives backed by Treasury explorations—might link digital IDs to programmable currencies, enforcing compliance through wallet controls and transaction tracking (White House 2025). In a world where your face, fingerprints, and blockchain credentials merge into one profile, the betrayal of freedom feels all too real.

MAHA as a Trojan Horse for MABA

In the landscape of American health policy under the second Trump administration, Robert F. Kennedy Jr.'s (RFK Jr.) appointment as U.S. Secretary of Health and Human Services in early 2025 marked a pivotal shift toward aggressive reform (HHS 2025). At the forefront of his agenda stands Make America Healthy Again (MAHA), a sweeping initiative aimed at tackling the nation's chronic disease epidemic through targeted interventions: scrutinizing harmful food additives, reevaluating vaccine safety frameworks, and fostering a culture of proactive wellness.

Yet, beneath this ostensibly populist banner of public health empowerment lies a more ambitious—and arguably insidious—blueprint: Make American Biotech Accelerate (MABA). RFK Jr. has framed MABA not as a standalone program but as an integral pillar of MAHA, positioning it as the engine for "unlocking American science" to deliver rapid medical breakthroughs. This integration raises questions about whether MAHA serves as a Trojan horse, cloaking the acceleration of biotech deregulation and corporate innovation under the guise of everyday health improvements.

RFK Jr. first publicly intertwined MAHA and MABA in a June 2025 statement, declaring: "The mission to Make America Healthy

Again (MAHA) includes MABA — Make American Biotech Accelerate. President Trump showed in his first term what happens when you unlock American science — breakthroughs happen fast. Now, we're going to do it again. We know the power of U.S. biotech.

"It's time to let it flourish — not tie it up in red tape, misalignment, and a process that gives the edge to foreign interests and large incumbents. We're clearing the path to transform great science into real cures, at lower costs, and better health for the American people. Life science and biotech are at the heart of that!" (Kennedy 2025). This rhetoric, repeated in congressional testimonies and public addresses throughout 2025, underscores a dual focus: dismantling bureaucratic hurdles within agencies like the FDA and HHS to spur domestic innovation, while countering global competitors, particularly China, in the biotech race.

Early MABA successes, such as expedited approvals for cultivated meat products from startups like Upside Foods, have been touted as proof of concept—demonstrating how regulatory streamlining can bring lab-grown alternatives to market faster. (USDA 2025).

Central to this MAHA-MABA nexus is RFK Jr.'s advocacy for wearable technology, which he has explicitly linked to broader health objectives. In a 2025 HHS briefing, he proclaimed that "wearables are a key to the MAHA agenda of making Americans healthy again," envisioning near-universal adoption within four years to democratize personal health data (Singh, Puyaan 2025). Through a high-profile HHS campaign, devices such as smartwatches, continuous glucose monitors, and fitness trackers have been promoted as tools for monitoring biometrics like steps, sleep patterns, stress levels, and heart rate variability.

RFK Jr. positions these as cost-effective alternatives to traditional pharmaceuticals—for instance, contrasting an $80 monthly subscription for a wearable-driven wellness program against the $1,000-plus cost of GLP-1 agonists like Ozempic. This push claims to empower individuals with "self-knowledge" for preventive care but also feeds directly into MABA's innovation ecosystem.

Here, the connections deepen: wearables under MAHA are paving the way for an expansive digital infrastructure, evolving into the Internet of Things (IoT), the Internet of Wearables (IoW), and ultimately the Internet of Everything (IoE). IoT encompasses the interconnected web of everyday devices exchanging data, but wearables represent a hyper-personalized entry point—the IoW—where clothing-embedded sensors, smart rings, and implantable trackers collect real-time physiological data.

RFK Jr.'s meetings with health tech startups, such as those developing AI-powered apps for predictive analytics, illustrate this trajectory. These tools aggregate wearable data, avowing to forecast health risks, prevent diseases, and customize interventions, like reversing Type 2 diabetes through AI-guided lifestyle adjustments monitored via glucose trends and activity logs. MABA accelerates this prioritizing biomanufacturing advancements—such as precision fermentation for synthetic proteins—and regulatory reforms that fast-track AI-integrated biotech, including genomic therapies tailored to individual datasets from wearables.

At the intersection of these elements lies AI-driven precision medicine, a cornerstone of the MAHA-MABA vision. By fusing wearable-generated big data with artificial intelligence, treatments move beyond one-size-fits-all models to hyper-personalized regimens informed by genetics, lifestyle, and environmental factors.

For example, AI algorithms could analyze a user's heart rate variability from a smartwatch alongside genomic sequencing to prescribe bespoke nutritional plans or early interventions for cardiovascular risks. MABA's emphasis on reducing "red tape" supports this by enabling faster approvals for AI tools in drug discovery and clinical trials, fostering a biotech boom where U.S. firms lead in creating "real cures" through data-rich ecosystems.

This convergence carries profound implications and risks. It promises enhanced preventive care, substantial cost savings for the healthcare system, and a shift toward wellness over sickness, but the proliferation of wearables under MAHA could normalize pervasive surveillance, laying the groundwork for an IoE where every aspect of human life— from personal habits to social interactions—is quantified and interconnected.

Data privacy concerns loom large: hacks on wearable platforms could expose sensitive health information, leading to misuse, control or discrimination by insurers or employers and advance bio-digital convergence agendas. The constant monitoring also risks over-medicalizing daily life, potentially fostering anxiety, hypochondria, or disorders like orthorexia, where an obsession with "healthy" metrics overrides balanced living. Ethical dilemmas arise from government-endorsed tech adoption, blurring lines between empowerment and control, especially if MABA's deregulatory zeal prioritizes corporate profits over equitable access.

While wearables and AI precision medicine align with MAHA's surface-level goals, their embedding within MABA reveals a deeper agenda: transforming public health into a conduit for biotech dominance and enabling synthetic biology advancement, which is conducive to bringing Nick Land's vision of "techno-plastic beings" to fruition.

MAHA may inadvertently—or deliberately—usher in an era where biotech acceleration, fueled by wearable data and IoT infrastructures, redefines not just medicine, but the very fabric of human connectivity and autonomy. As Klaus Schwab says, "The Fourth Industrial Revolution is not only changing what we are doing, but also who we are".

Conclusion: The Dictatorship Realized

In the shadows of this scientific dictatorship, the pillars of surveillance, Palantir's unyielding gaze, universal digital IDs, and the MAHA-MABA deception converge to forge an unbreakable chain around human freedom. What was promised as a restoration of American sovereignty under MAGA — if left unchecked — is devolving into a technocratic Sov-Corp, where citizens are commodified data streams, dissent is algorithmically silenced, and autonomy is sacrificed at the altar of efficiency.

As we mark the one-year milestone of the 2024 election, the betrayal is complete. If we don't act now, we risk the republic being supplanted by a machine of control, orchestrated by elites like Thiel, Musk, and RFK Jr. Awakening to this reality is our last defense—lest we awaken too late in a world where liberty is but a forgotten code.

References

Abdella, Battou NIST. n.d. "Smart Infrastructure and Manufacturing." National Institute of Standards and Technology. March 26, 2025 https://www.nist.gov/programs-projects/smart-infrastructure-and-manufacturing.

ACLU. 2025. "Surveillance Company Flock Now Using AI to Report Us to Police if It Thinks Our Movement Patterns Are Suspicious." American Civil Liberties Union. https://www.aclu.org/news/national-security/surveillance-company-flock-now-using-ai-to-report-us-to-police-if-it-thinks-our-movement-patterns-are-suspicious.

Adorno, Theodor W. 1994. The Stars Down to Earth and Other Essays on the Irrational in Culture. Edited by Stephen Crook. London: Routledge.

Akin, William E. 1977. Technocracy and the American Dream: The Technocrat Movement, 1900-1941. Berkeley: University of California Press.

Arcadian AI. 2025. "Video Surveillance in the USA 2025: Trends, Statistics, Privacy Concerns, and the Future of AI Monitoring." Arcadian AI. https://www.arcadian.ai/blogs/blogs/video-surveillance-in-the-usa-2025-trends-statistics-privacy-concerns-and-the-future-of-ai-monitoring.

Berger, Eric. 2024. "Starlink Set to Hit $11.8 Billion Revenue in 2025, Boosted by Military Contracts." SpaceNews, December 16. https://spacenews.com/starlink-set-to-hit-11-8-billion-revenue-in-2025-boosted-by-military-contracts/.

Clearview AI. 2025. "Principles." Clearview AI. https://www.clearview.ai/principles.

CompaniesMarketCap. 2025. "Palantir (PLTR) - Revenue." CompaniesMarketCap. https://companiesmarketcap.com/palantir/revenue/.

Ellul, Jacques. 1954. The Technological Society. Translated by John Wilkinson. New York: Vintage Books.

Godkin, Edwin L. 1898. Unforeseen Tendencies of Democracy. Boston: Houghton Mifflin.

Amin, Lucas; Geoghegan, Peter. 2025. "UK Government Withholding Details of Palantir Contract." Democracy for Sale, May 24. https://democracyforsale.substack.com/p/uk-government-withholding-details.

Hatmaker, Taylor March 27, 2019. "Palantir Wins $800 Million Contract to Build the US Army's Next Battlefield Software System." TechCrunch, March 27. https://techcrunch.com/2019/03/27/palantir-army-contract-dcgs-a/.

Hemmadi, Murad. The Logic. 2025. "The Defence Department Had a $14M Contract with Palantir for Data Processing and Analytics." The Logic, September 18. https://thelogic.co/news/palantir-department-of-national-defence-contract-canada/.

HHS. 2025. "Make America Healthy Again (MAHA)." U.S. Department of Health and Human Services. https://www.hhs.gov/maha/index.html.

Huxley, Aldous. 1932. Brave New World. London: Chatto & Windus.

Kennedy, Robert F Jr. 2025 https://x.com/SecKennedy/status/1936199106936160516

Macrotrends. 2025. "Palantir Technologies Revenue 2019-2025 | PLTR." Macrotrends. https://www.macrotrends.net/stocks/charts/PLTR/palantir-technologies/revenue.

Temoshok, David (NIST), Diana Proud-Madruga (Electrosoft), Yee-Yin Choong et al.

NIST. July 2025. SP 800-63-4, Digital Identity Guidelines. Gaithersburg, MD: National Institute of Standards and Technology. https://csrc.nist.gov/pubs/sp/800/63/4/final.

NPR. 2025. "RFK Jr. Says Americans Were Healthier When His Uncle Was President—But Life Expectancy Tells a Different Story." NPR, June 8. https://www.npr.org/2025/06/06/nx-s1-5399616/rfk-jr-life-expectancy-chronic-disease-maha.

Train Grok AI. Here's How to Stop It." PCMag, August 27. https://www.pcmag.com/how-to/your-tweets-x-posts-train-elon-musk-grok-ai-how-to-stop-it-opt-out.

Singh, Puyaan. Reuters. June 24th 2025. "US Health Secretary Kennedy Says HHS to Launch Campaign to Encourage Wearable Devices." Reuters, June 24. https://www.reuters.com/business/healthcare-pharmaceuticals/us-health-secretary-kennedy-says-hhs-launch-campaign-encourage-wearable-devices-2025-06-24/.

Smyth, William Henry. 1919. "Technocracy." Industrial Management 57: 208-212.

Smyth, William Henry. 1921. Technocracy: First, Second and Third Series. Social Universals. Berkeley, CA: Self-published.

Subin, Samantha. 2025. "Palantir Lands $10 Billion Army Software and Data Contract." CNBC, August 1. https://www.cnbc.com/2025/08/01/palantir-lands-10-billion-army-software-and-data-contract.html.

Temoshok, David (NIST), Diana Proud-Madruga (Electrosoft), Yee-Yin Choong et al.

NIST. 2025. SP 800-63-4, Digital Identity Guidelines. Gaithersburg, MD: National Institute of Standards and Technology. https://csrc.nist.gov/pubs/sp/800/63/4/final.

Tesla. n.d. "AI & Robotics." Tesla. https://www.tesla.com/AI.

TSA. 2025. "REAL ID Frequently Asked Questions." Transportation Security Administration. https://www.tsa.gov/real-id/real-id-faqs.

TSA. n.d. "Participating States and Eligible Digital IDs." Transportation Security Administration. https://www.tsa.gov/digital-id/participating-states.

USDA. 2025. "Human Food Made with Cultured Animal Cells Inventory." U.S. Department of Agriculture. https://www.cfsanappsexternal.fda.gov/scripts/fdcc/?set=animalcellculturefoods.

Wells, H. G. 1938. World Brain. London: Methuen & Co.

White House. 2025. "Strengthening American Leadership in Digital Financial Technology." The White House, January 23. https://www.whitehouse.gov/presidential-actions/2025/01/strengthening-american-leadership-in-digital-financial-technology/

Chapter 10

The New International Economic Order

When the Trilateral Commission was created in 1973 by David Rockefeller and Zbigniew Brzezinski, its stated tag line was to create a New International Economic Order (NIEO). Looking backward and forward, we can see:

- The stripping of natural assets from private and national hands

- The creation of resource management system to create profits for the holders

- The creation of a new type of monetary system based on assets, rather than on debt.

- The establishment of Technocracy as the method of management.

In 1973, David Rockefeller's dilemma was money. As the Chairman of Chase Manhattan Bank (Now, JP Morgan Chase), Rockefeller had piles of money but no resources. In the end, he saw the end of debt-based money, all of which was just fiat currency. During the 70's, he grew Chase Manhattan into a international behemoth and became a model for the globalization of American financial institutions.

Meanwhile, Brzezinski laid the foundation for Technocracy and all of its guiding principles, and spread it around the world in lock-step with the global banking system. China was the first nation to fully embrace Technocracy under Brzezinski's tenure as National Security Advisor under President Jimmy Carter. Thereafter, he oversaw the birthing of Sustainable Development (a resource-based economic system modeled after 1930s Technocracy) under Agenda21 at the United Nations.

The die was cast. Since then, the whole world has been captured by Agenda21, with its anti-private property policies at the heart. All other U.N. policies of Sustainable Development have served to drive people off their land: food and agriculture polices, water polices, health and medical polices, etc.

Now that fiat currencies have run their course and the implosion of debt is at hand, the global banking cartel (fashioned by Rockefeller in the 1970s and 1980s) is pivoting, even careening into the digitization and tokenization of assets, in preparation for launching the NIEO.

The scale of land acquisition is staggering. Data from the Land Matrix and World Bank, indicate that hundreds of millions of acres—on par with the combined land area of India and Argentina—are now held, managed, or financially leveraged by international investors, sovereign funds, and development banks between 1973 and 2025. The overall trend shows accelerating consolidation of land and resource control into global financial systems, with private capital, public investment arms, and UN-related NGOs intersecting with new Technocratic governance models. (Fian 2025)

What will the NIEO look like? When the World Economic Forum suggested in 2021 that "by 2030, you will own nothing", they furiously backpedalled, stating they "consistently emphasize *responsible*, *transparent*, and *inclusive* ownership, both for individuals and businesses." That's another way of saying that you will indeed own nothing when its over. (Reuters 2021)

Under the aegis of Executive Order 14178 of January 23, 2025, the policy document, "Strengthening American Leadership in Digital Financial Technology," Secretary of Commerce Howard Lutnick clearly identified commercial real estate, mineral rights, and federal land leases as “tokenizable asset classes” within a forthcoming government framework aimed at integrating blockchain into economic data management. His stated rationale centered on modernization, transparency, and liquidity creation for otherwise illiquid public holdings. (Sacks 2025)

Lutnick subsequently went on national TV outlets to state the value of those assets were in the range of $500 trillion. Is this enough to wipe all debt from government and citizens alike? As of late 2025, the total U.S. dollar-denominated debt across all major sectors—federal, state and local government, corporations, and households exceeds $77 trillion, according to the Federal Reserve’s *Financial Accounts of the United States (Z.1, 2025 Q1)* and related Treasury and Congressional data.

Is this Trump's Golden Age?

Tokens, tokens everywhere

With the Federal Reserve temporarily on the sidelines, Trump's Technocratic crypto wizards have succeeded in privatizing our monetary payment system. But, they have gone far beyond just payments: they are lining up to tokenize all assets as well. The Fed could never have achieved this in the first place because it was only concerned with corralling the payments system. Now we are on the verge of a duplicitous payments and associated asset system that are based on the same tokenization process.

By late 2025, many of the world’s largest financial and technology firms are actively investing in asset tokenization, transitioning real-world assets such as treasuries, real estate, and commodities onto blockchain infrastructures. (Chernikova 2025)

The leaders of the tokenization craze won't surprise you: BlackRock, Franklin Templeton, Goldman Sachs and J.P. Morgan, Chase. Howard Lutnick's old firm, Cantor Fitzgerald (CF), is now run by his sons. CF owns a five percent share of Tether, which plays the leading role in the stablecoin market. With several acquisitions in 2025, CF has emerged as the institutional backbone of tokenized capital markets. In short, the titans of Wall Street and global banking are gearing up for a frenzied tokenization of everything on the planet.

Islamic Finance and Banking Takes A Seat

As of 2025, Islamic banking serves roughly 1.8 billion people, representing twenty-five percent of the world's population, primarily across Muslim-majority regions in the Middle East, South and Southeast Asia, and parts of Africa. Islamic Banking relies on core principles of Sharia law, outlawing debt or usury. (Khalafalla 2025)

Because Islamic banking relies exclusively on assets, it represents an asset-based economic system. Islamic banking and finance creates, sells and services products that are in strict accordance with Sharia. In the Islamic culture, it is referred to as “Sharia finance” and covers the practices of banking, investment, bonds, loans, brokerage, etc.

There is a dark side to Sharia, the legal and judicial system of Islam that is brutally imposed on many Islamic countries in the middle east. It is the specific embodiment of the totalitarian ideology practiced by the Taliban, Iranian Mullahs and Saudi Wahhabis.

Sharia demands total and unquestioned submission. Its subjects are told that Sharia is given by Allah and that whatever befalls them (good or bad) is Allah’s will. To question a judgment under Sharia (right or wrong) is to question Sharia itself and will only bring harsher punishment. If a person receives harsh punishment for something they didn’t do, the rationale is that Allah could and would have prevented it if that had been his will. This fatalistic and deterministic approach allows Sharia rulers to get away with virtually any thing that enters their head. (Wood 2025)

Western bankers embraced Sharia Banking starting in 2006, offering compliant products like:

- **Mudarabah** – A partnership where one party provides capital and the other provides management; profits are shared, losses borne by the investor.
- **Musharakah** – Joint venture where partners share both profit and loss according to their contribution.
- **Murabahah** – Cost-plus sale; the bank buys goods and resells them at a markup.
- **Salam** – Advance payment for future delivery of commodities.
- **Istisna'** – Commissioned manufacturing or construction contract with deferred delivery.
- **Ijarah** – Islamic leasing; transfer of asset use, not ownership, in exchange for rent.
- **Sukuk** – Islamic bonds representing ownership in underlying assets.

Since 2006, global banks like JP Morgan Chase, Goldman Sachs, Citigroup, HSBC, Deutsche Bank and Morgan Stanley all have dedicated Islamic finance divisions. The normalization of Islamic products has been so complete that Islamic finance is no longer seen as foreign or exotic. It has been rebranded as "ethical finance," "ESG investing," and "sustainable banking." By wrapping Sharia compliance in the language of environmental and social responsibility, Western institutions have made Islamic finance palatable to non-Muslim customers who might otherwise object to financing structures based on religious law. (Wood 2007)

These Western banks have done for Islam what it could never do on its own: give legitimacy to Sharia and infiltrate it into the fabric of western society.

Islamic Leadership in FinTech

The Islamic world aspires to lead the Financial Technology (FinTech) sector that is pushing AI, blockchain, tokenization and digital ID systems.

Their financial institutions are integrating AI, blockchain, and digital banking platforms to enhance Sharia-compliant services. Emerging Islamic neobanks and startups like INSIFR, as well as crypto exchanges such as Rain and CoinMENA licensed in Bahrain, are introducing AI-driven financial management tools, blockchain-based sukuk (Islamic bonds), and halal P2P lending and crowdfunding platforms.

The adoption of FinTech is a major factor of the exponential growth. This headline in June 2025, "Global Islamic Finance Grows 14.9%, Reaches US$3.9 Trillion in Total Assets", underscores the point.

Since 2023, global and regional leaders have positioned the Middle East as a strategic crossroad for digital finance governance and innovation. Conferences in Dubai, Riyadh, Manama, and Cairo now act as global meeting points for regulators, banks, and tech investors, reinforcing the GCC's ambition to be a nexus of digital finance modernization bridging Asia, Africa, and Europe. (Fintechnews 2024)

In short, leadership in Middle Eastern fintech is state-supported, regulator-coordinated, and entrepreneur-driven, turning the Gulf Cooperation Council (GCC) into a world-class testing ground for digital banking, AI-finance integration, and Islamic-compliant fintech models that blend faith-based governance with next-generation financial technology. The GCC is a regional, intergovernmental, political, and economic union of six Arab countries: Bahrain, Kuwait, Oman, Qatar, Saudi Arabia, and the United Arab Emirates.

The Great Economic Flip

If structured around transparency, shared ownership, and value-linked assets, a Western FinTech-enabled asset-based system is not only compatible with Islamic banking but potentially synergistic, providing the technological foundation to scale global Sharia-compliant finance. The fusion could result in a post-debt monetary architecture that combines Western efficiency with Islamic ethics and stability. (Day 2025)

This partly explains why President Trump, since his inauguration on January 23, 2025, has negotiated over $2 trillion in economic and financial agreements with Islamic banking nations across the Gulf and Southeast Asia:

- **Saudi Arabia** – $600 billion for energy, AI, green tech, infrastructure, and joint investment partnerships

- **UAE** – $700 billion for FinTech, defense, renewable energy, sovereign fund co-investment

- **Qatar** – $700 billion for Digital economy, LNG infrastructure, and sovereign wealth flows

Note in that each instance, you see AI, tech, FinTech, digital economy. Also note the emphasis on sovereign wealth funds! All of these initiatives emphasize asset-backed industrial investment, which aligns structurally with Islamic finance principles of real-economy value creation rather than debt issuance .

Needless to say, the scale of these deals is historically unprecedented. It also marks a tectonic shift of economic policy and acceptance and/or validation of Islamic finance principles and Fin-Tech.

On the day when debt is declared dead in America, it will mark the beginning of the New International Economic Order, to wit:

- The final accumulation assets will commence by oligarchs, their companies and sovereign wealth firms.
- The bio-digital id system will be revealed immediately
- All assets with value will be tokenized for global trading
- Mopping up the remaining lose ends of the resulting debt mess will be swift
- Private property will become a memory.

The words of Zbigniew Brzezinski, the modern architect of Technocracy and the New International Economic Order, are reminiscent for this day and age. He wrote this in 1973:

> *"Tension is unavoidable as man strives to assimilate the new into the framework of the old. For a time the established framework resiliently integrates the new by adapting it in a more familiar shape. But at some point the old framework becomes overloaded. The newer input can no longer be redefined into traditional forms, and eventually it asserts itself with compelling force. Today, though, the old framework of international politics – with their spheres of influence, military alliances between nation-states, the fiction of Sovereignty, doctrinal conflicts arising from nineteenth century crises – is clearly no longer compatible with reality." (Brzezinski 1973)*

If you read Brzezinski's book, *Between Two Ages: America's Role in the Technetronic Order*, you will see him looking backward and forward, seeing the day in the future when his New International Economic Order will appear.

Fast forward to 2023, when another Trilateral Commission member stood up at the annual plenary meeting in New Delhi, India and declared,

> *"Three decades of globalization — defined as integrated, free-market based and deflationary — has been replaced by what will be a multi-decade period of globalization defined as fragmented, not-free-market-based but industrial-policy based and structurally inflationary.* ***This year, 2023, is Year One of this new global order."*** *(Wood 2023)*

That day is upon us!

References

Brzezinski, Zbigniew, *Between Two Ages: America's Role in the Technetronic Era* (New York: Viking Press, 1973), p. 246.

FIAN International, "Global Land Grab Highlights Growing Inequality", June 3, 2025. (https://www.fian.org/en/global-land-grab-highlights-growing-inequality-and-need-for-reform/)

Chernikova, Anastasia, "Real-World Asset Tokenization Hits $24 Billion As Wall Street Bets Big", Forbes, June 23, 2025. (https://www.forbes.com/sites/digital-assets/2025/06/20/real-world-asset-tokenization-hits-24-billion-as-wall-street-bets-big/)

Dey, Debashis, Ola Sanni, "Islamic Finance 2.0 : Innovation, Tokenisation, and the Evolution of

Sukuk Markets in the GCC, White Case, June 4, 2025. (https://www.whitecase.com/insight-alert/islamic-finance-20-innovation-tokenisation-evolution-sukuk-markets-gcc)

Fintechnews Middle East, "Top 10 Fintech Events in Saudi Arabia in 2025", December 23, 2024. (https://fintechnews.ae/23452/fintech-saudi-arabia/top-10-fintech-events-in-saudi-arabia-in-2025/)

Khalafalla, Dr. Khalid, "Islamic Finance Development Report 2025", LSEG Data & Analytics, Q1 2025. (https://www.lseg.com/content/dam/data-analytics/en_us/documents/reports/lseg-islamic-finance-development-indicator-2025.pdf)

Reuters, "The World Economic Forum does not have a stated goal to have people own nothing by 2030", February 25, 2021. (https://www.reuters.com/article/world/fact-check-the-world-economic-forum-does-not-have-a-stated-goal-to-have-people-idUSKBN2AP2SP/)

Sacks, David, "Strengthening American Leadership in Digital Financial Technology", January 23, 2025. (https://www.whitehouse.gov/wp-content/uploads/2025/07/digital-Assets-Report-EO14178.pdf)

Wood, Patrick, "Trilateral Commission Declares '2023 is Year One of this new global order'", Technocracy News & Trends, 2023. (https://www.technocracy.news/endgame-unleashed-trilateral-commission-declares-2023-is-year-one-of-this-new-global-order/)

Wood, Patrick, "Global Banks Adopting Islam", Technocracy News & Trends, May 5, 2007. (https://www.technocracy.news/flashback-2007-global-banks-adopting-islam/)

Wood, Patrick, "Own Nothing? The Great Islamic Finance Convergence", Technocracy News & Trends, September 8,

2025. (https://www.technocracy.news/own-nothing-the-great-islamic-finance-convergence/)

Chapter 11

The Players

This is a short list of Technocrats influencing policy in the Federal Administration. It is not exhaustive, but it gives you an idea of who these people are. We are including this as a Chapter instead of an Appendix, to maximize understanding.

John Ackerly - Data privacy leader, former White House policy advisor, ex-strategic planner at U.S. Commerce; business degrees from Williams College and Harvard.

Sam Altman - The venture capitalist CEO of OpenAI, but hasn't contributed one line of code to OpenAI.

Scott Bessent – Secretary of the Treasury; pivotal in driving crypto and digital asset innovation policy. Former CIO of the Soros Fund.

Riccardo Biasini - Formerly of Tesla and The Boring Company, served as senior adviser at OPM, notably implementing new government-wide email systems.

Christian Brose – President of Anduril. A back-seat advisor of defense policy and modernization.

Steve Davis - A close aide of Mr. Musk for two decades, is effectively the leader of DOGE.

Delali Dzirasa – Founder & CEO, Fearless. An impact-driven tech executive, Dzirasa works at the intersection of government digital services and diversity advocacy, supporting innovative software solutions for federal agencies and professional development for underrepresented talent.

Larry Ellison - Currently the richest billionaire on Earth, the co-founder of Oracle Corporation, and instigator of the Stargate Project.

Luke Farritor - A Musk associate at SpaceX, and a computer scientist who dropped out of college to work at the GSA.

Amy Gleason - Acting DOGE Administrator, oversees DOGE structure, reporting to the White House Chief of Staff.

Bo Hines – Executive Director of the White House Crypto Council; coordinates interagency and Congressional collaboration on digital asset regulations.

Nicole Hollander - Led efforts to shrink the government's physical and operational footprint, especially within the General Services Administration. Managed government real estate strategies within the GSA.

Michael Kratsios - Director of the White House Office of Science and Technology Policy, leading the "AI Action Plan" and major initiatives to boost American AI competitiveness, export AI, and modernize federal digital infrastructure.

Tom Krause - Former Cloud Software Group CEO, managed the Treasury Department's payment systems and led DOGE budget-cutting efforts at Treasury.

Nick Land - a British philosopher, who coined the term Dark Enlightenment and *accelerationism*, and whose radical work in the 1990s and association with the Cybernetic Culture Research Unit evolved into key anti-egalitarian, anti-democratic ideas that now undergird the Dark Enlightenment; he emphasizes techno-capitalist acceleration and critiques Enlightenment humanism.

Palmer Luckey – Founder of Anduril, back-seat advisor to the Trump Administration on defense polities.

Howard Lutnick – Secretary of Commerce; oversees tech export controls and digital asset market supervision. Former Chairman and CEO of Cantor Fitzgerald L.P. and BGC Partners, Inc.

Hester Peirce – SEC Commissioner; heads the Crypto Task Force, crafting practical regulatory frameworks for digital assets.

Douglas Matty - Chief Digital and AI Officer, U.S. Department of Defense. With 30+ years in military and technical roles, Matty leads the Pentagon's AI and digital transformation agenda.

Bruce Mehlman - Founder of Mehlman Consulting and noted policy influencer in tech and telecom, Mehlman shapes public discourse and strategy via high-level consultations and widely read policy briefings,

Ed Morche - CEO of GTT, leading advances in telecommunications and digital solutions vital to D.C.'s tech-driven policy agenda and infrastructure overhaul.

Elon Musk - Co-founder of PayPal with Peter Thiel, CEO of SpaceX, X.ai, and Tesla, former policy advisor to President Trump, major government contractor. His grandfather was head of the Technocracy, Inc. movement in Canada during the 1930s and 1940s.

Michael Obadal - Senior director at Anduril, serves as Under Secretary of the Army, the second-highest civilian post.

Jim O'Neil – Acting director of the CDC, former CEO of the Thiel Foundation

Lakshmi Raman - Chief AI Officer, CIA. Raman is transforming agency operations by integrating AI agents for automation while establishing new ethical and governance standards for sensitive intelligence applications.

Adam Ramada - DOGE liaison between Musk's engineers and political appointees in the government.

Vivek Ramaswamy - Originally announced as Musk's DOGE co-leader but reportedly stepped back from formal leadership; still influential in the network.

David Sacks - Newly appointed federal "AI and Cryptocurrency Czar," Sacks is a prominent tech investor and member of the "Paypal Mafia," driving national strategies around artificial intelligence, crypto assets, and digital policy.

Amanda Scales - Previously with Musk at xAI, became chief of staff at the Office of Personnel Management (OPM), overseeing federal HR functions.

Cenk Sidar – CEO, Enquire.AI. Sidar combines global expertise and AI to transform policy decision support and investment analysis, recognized in D.C. for revolutionizing expert knowledge networks.

Thomas Shedd - The Director of Technology Transformation Services (TTS) and Deputy Commissioner of the Federal Acquisition Service at the U.S. General Services Administration (GSA), as well as Chief Information Officer at the U.S. Department of Labor (DOL).

Brad Smith - functioned as a chief of staff for DOGE during the presidential transition and has led the team with Steve Davis.

Trae Stephens – Co-founder of Anduril and partner of Thiel's Founders Fund. Advised the President and national security team on restructuring U.S. defense spending and modernization.

Peter Thiel - Venture capitalist, PayPal co-founder, Palantir co-Founder, and mentor to J.D. Vance, Thiel actively advises the administration on emerging technology, national security, and US-Silicon Valley industrial policy. An accelerationist voice, he welcomes rapid tech-driven change over gradual reforms.

Mark T. Uyeda – Acting Chairman of the Securities and Exchange Commission (SEC); launched the SEC's Crypto Task Force.

J.D. Vance - His rise in politics and business was significantly shaped by Peter Thiel, the billionaire tech investor who mentored Vance, employed him in his Silicon Valley venture firm, and later provided multi-million-dollar backing for Vance's Senate campaign and political ascent. Currently, the Vice President of the U.S.

Russ Vought – Chief architect of Project 2025, now Director of OMB (Office of Management and Budget) and supports Christian Nationalism. Called the *Shadow President* by many inside Washington, DC.

Kevin Weil - Chief Product Officer, OpenAI. Weil drives agentic AI—AI tools that autonomously perform real-world tasks. He recently became a senior advisor to the U.S. Army, bringing together expertise from big tech and government.

Doug Wilson -The informal leader and key inspiration behind the "TheoBro" movement—a network of ultraconservative, mostly millennial men advocating Christian nationalism and biblical law as the basis for American governance. Many TheoBros are in the tech industry.

Curtis Yarvin (aka Mencius Moldbug) - is an American political theorist and Silicon Valley software developer, best known as a founder of the neo-reactionary "Dark Enlightenment" movement, advocating for the replacement of democracy with a technocratic monarchy led by a CEO-like figure.

Mark Zuckerberg - Co-founder of Facebook, now Meta Platforms, Inc.

Epilogue

The greatest betrayal in human history has just taken place. It has strip-mined our rights as free citizens, while delivering us into a digital gulag. Is this truly the end of the "American Experiment?" We didn't ask for it. We didn't vote for it. We weren't consulted, nor did we give informed consent. Instead, we were tricked, deceived, and gaslighted at every turn.

The first expression of Americana came with the Declaration of Independence in 1776:

> *We hold these truths to be self-evident, that all men are created equal, that they are endowed by their Creator with certain unalienable Rights, that among these are Life, Liberty and the pursuit of Happiness.*

The Virginia Declaration of Rights was also written in 1976, and it defined the *right to life, liberty, and property.*

Life, liberty, the pursuit of happiness, and property were all considered unalienable rights given by God, not man. Technocrats deny the existence of God; therefore, He can't grant rights to anyone. The mechanistic worldview of Technocracy posits that humans are merely a random collection of atoms and molecules. If you have any rights at all, they will be given and taken away by Technocratic overlords.

Repudiating Technocracy

Decisive action is required. Start by wrapping a guard around your mind. Repudiate mechanistic thinking. Take everything as propaganda until proven otherwise. Speak up; your voice is your only voice. Only you can think for yourself. If you sleep, you will soon become a casualty.

Don't fall into Peter Thiel's trap: "Whenever people think you can just muddle through, you're probably set up for some kind of disaster." (Tyler, 2024)

Technocrats are not invincible. Exploit their vulnerabilities, weaknesses, and blind spots wherever you can. When you are in a doctor's office, talk about abuses of AI in claim mismanagement. When you attend church, true your faith by pointing out extra-Biblical doctrines. When you are at work, tell your bosses and co-workers that AI delivers "slopwork," where passable work done by AI increases the workload for others.

When you sense that someone above you wants you to play a role in their technocratic narrative, dig your heels in and don't do it!

Think Local, Act Local

Your audience and most significant influence is local - not state, regional, or national. Be that influence.

Most towns and cities have multiple boards and city councils. These are your neighbors, subject to local influence and direction. Engage with them with practical discourse, appealing to them to put protective barriers around your home, local businesses, and the broader community.

When you see outside consultants brought in to manage projects like General Plans, Sustainable Development projects, or Climate Action plans, run them out of town. You are paying your city leaders to do the planning for your city or town, not out-of-town consultants who don't know anything about where you live, and couldn't care less.

What Does It Mean To Be Human?

The *Technocracy Study Course,* written in 1934, made an odd statement in its introduction: "Technocracy declares that this Continent has a rendezvous with Destiny." Whose Destiny?

With biting cynicism, the writers of the Study Course threw Christianity under the bus as stupid, irrelevant, and standing in the way of Destiny:

> *Dogs, horses, cows, and monkeys may have evolved from lower life forms, but man - never! Man, after all, had a soul and a conscience. He could reason and could discern the difference between right and wrong. He was something above and apart from the brute beasts of the field. While this fight lasted for a period of 30 to 40 years, as usual the facts won out against tradition, and human beings, much as it hurt their egotism to have to do so, were so far removed from the pedestal upon which they had originally imagined themselves to be, that at last they were obliged to admit blood kinship with the other members of the animal kingdom.* (Scott & Hubbert 1934)

This mechanistic worldview persists to the present day. If you are just an animal like a cow or a horse, you are only as valuable for the milk you produce or the freight you can haul. When your productive functions cease, you become a "useless eater" and a burden to society.

The term "useless eater", by the way, originated in technocratic Nazi Germany as a dehumanizing label to describe individuals with disabilities, the chronically ill, or others whom the regime categorized as "life unworthy of life" due to their perceived lack of economic contribution. (Sample 2022)

To Technocrats, human problems exist to be solved; minds are to be engineered; values reduced to utility. Sentience, agency, and conscience raise little more than procedural questions: Can they be measured? Can they be controlled?

Technocracy doesn't allow for free will, moral agency, or human dignity. As such, to the Technocrat, you certainly don't have unalienable rights given by God to "Life, Liberty, and the pursuit of Happiness" that were mentioned in the Declaration of Independence.

It's no wonder that so many people have concluded that Technocracy is not just pseudo-human, but it is **flat-out anti-human**.

So, the war against humanity boils down to this: do you have a right to be human, or not?

To be human means possessing qualities that distinguish people from animals, machines, and other entities — encompassing not just biological characteristics but complex psychological, social, and philosophical dimensions as well. Humanity is marked by self-awareness, rationality, moral judgment, creativity, emotional depth, and the capacity for language and culture.

To the Christian worldview, man was created in the image of God, endowed with conscience, a moral compass, and free will to choose between good and evil, between eternal life and judgment based on a personal relationship with Christ, or not. Nevertheless, each human on earth has intrinsic worth, not based on contribution but on existence itself.

The age-old questions of life are uniquely human,

- Who am I?
- Why am I here?

- Where am I going?
- What is the meaning of life?

No Technocrat has the right to answer these for you, but they would be happy to gaslight you to the contrary.

Above all, hang onto your humanity!

References

Sample, Emily, The Hunger Plan: The Holocaust, Resource Scarcity, and Preventing Genocide in a Changing Climate, George Mason University, July 7, 2022.

Scott & Hubbert, Technocracy Study Course, Technocracy, Inc., 1934.

Tyler, Cowen, My excellent Conversation with Peter Thiel, Marginal Revolution, April 18, 2024.

Index

Also by Patrick Wood

Trilaterals over Washington, Vol I & II

Globalization and the Crucible of Global Banking

Technocracy Rising: The Trojan Horse of Global Transformation

Technocracy: The Hard Road To World Order

The Evil Twins of Technocracy & Transhumanism

The Genesis of Modern Globalization (1978-1979)

---

https://www.Technocracy.News

Courtenay Turner

https://www.CourtenayTurner.com

Made in the USA
Coppell, TX
15 February 2026

71346734R00095